OF GUNS AND MULES

D. LAWRENCE-YOUNG

Copyright © D. Lawrence-Young
Jerusalem 2010/5769

All rights reserved. No part of this publication may be translated, reproduced, stored in a retrieval system or transmitted, in any form or by any means, electronic, mechanical, photocopying, recording or otherwise, without express written permission from the publishers.

Typesetting and Cover Design by S. Kim Glassman
Author Photograph: Douglas Guthrie

ISBN: 978-965-229-457-9
1 3 5 7 9 8 6 4 2

Gefen Publishing House, Ltd.	Gefen Books
6 Hatzvi Street	600 Broadway
Jerusalem 94386, Israel	Lynbrook, NY 11563, USA
972-2-538-0247	1-800-477-5257
orders@gefenpublishing.com	orders@gefenpublishing.com

www.gefenpublishing.com

Printed in Israel   *Send for our free catalogue*

*To my wife, Beverley,
who, on more than one occasion,
saved this book from accidentally being deleted,
and also to my children, Vered, Nadav and
Ya'acov, and grandchildren, Oz and Zur.*

*Also to Marion Lupu and Kezia Raffel Pride,
my very meticulous but supportive editors.*

This is a work of fiction. Although based on historical events, no character or event in this book, with the exception of historical persons, is real, and any resemblance to real persons is unintentional. All dialogue in this work is a product of the author's imagination, including that of real-life historical or public figures.

Other Books by D. Lawrence-Young

Tolpuddle: A Novel

Gunpowder, Treason & Plot: A Novel

Of Plots & Passions: A Thousand Years of Devious Deeds

Communicating in English (ed.)

Contents

Acknowledgments ix
Introduction xi

Chapter One
    Deportation 1

Chapter Two
    The Zion Mule Corps 11

Chapter Three
    David Levi, ZMC 19

Chapter Four
    To Cape Helles 25

Chapter Five
    Gallipoli 39

Chapter Six
    January 1916: Evacuation 51

Chapter Seven
    July 1917: The Jewish Legion 63

Chapter Eight
    From London back to Alexandria 77

Chapter Nine
    Eretz Israel Again! 83

Chapter Ten
    Action on the East Bank 93

Chapter Eleven
    Umm Es Shert and Es Salt 105

Chapter Twelve
    Armistice and Demobilization 121

Afterword 139
About the Author 147

Acknowledgments

Although this book is a work of historical fiction, it is based on events that really happened in Palestine, Egypt, Gallipoli, Italy and England during the First World War. My research included talking to interested people, visiting museums and historic sites, as well as consulting various books and articles. The museums I visited included Bet Hagedudim, the museum devoted to the ZMC and Jewish Legion, near Netanya, Israel; the very impressive Australian War Museum in Canberra, Australia; and I also toured the Gallipoli peninsula battlefields in Turkey.

The books I consulted included:

The Hebrew Battalions: Letters by Izhak Ben-Zvi
    (Israel's second president) translated from the
    Hebrew by Taffi Baker and Margalit Benaya
    (Jerusalem: Yad Izhak Ben-Zvi, 1969)

Soldiers in Judea: Stories and Vignettes of the Jewish Legion
    by Roman Freulich
    (New York: Herzl Press, 1964)

The Jewish Legion in World War I
    by Yigal Elam [Hebrew]
    (Tel Aviv, 1973)

With the Zionists in Gallipoli
    by Lieutenant Colonel J.H. Patterson DSO
    (London: Hutchinson & Co., 1916)

Gallipoli, 1915: Frontal Assault on Turkey
    by Philip J. Haythornwaite
    (London: Osprey, 1991)

Allenby
    by Brian Gardner
    (London: Cassell, 1965)

The Great War: Perspectives on The First World War
    edited by Robert Cowley
    (New York: Random House, 2003)

I also found the following articles which Bet Hagedudim kindly gave me to be very helpful:

"New Light on the Founding of the Legion in 1917"
    by Y. Finklestone

"The Jewish Legion"
    by Dr. J. Schechtman

"The Exiles' Camps in Egypt"
    by Dr. H.H. Ben-Sasson

"The Idea of the Hebrew Legions"
    by Dr. H.H. Ben-Sasson

"The Volunteer Movement among American Jews"
    by Dr. H.H. Ben-Sasson

Even though I combed through the above material very carefully, if any historical or military mistakes come to light, then I alone am responsible. I would be very pleased to hear from readers through my e-mail: dlwhy08@gmail.com.

D. Lawrence-Young,
Jerusalem, Israel
July 2009

Introduction

The Ottoman Empire, later known as the Turkish Empire, stretched from Greece in the west through to the coasts of modern Saudi Arabia and Yemen in the east. It included much of modern-day Greece, Turkey, Israel, Jordan, Syria and Iraq. It began in the early fourteenth century and lasted for about six hundred years, ending in the winter of 1917 when General Allenby ousted the Turkish army from Palestine and the Middle East. The Ottoman rulers divided the biblical Eretz Israel east of the River Jordan into four *sanjak*s (districts): Jerusalem, Gaza, Nablus and Safed.

The Jewish population took an active and positive part in the daily political and economic life of the empire, and many Spanish Jews who fled the Inquisition were welcomed. As a result, the empire became the center of Sepharadi culture, and in general, the Jews lived peaceful and secure lives. This situation contrasted to that of much of the rest of Europe and Russia where they suffered many major political and social restrictions, such as living in ghettos.

Today only a few examples of Ottoman buildings and remains may be found in Israel. The most well known examples that still stand include the wall that surrounds the Old City of Jerusalem, built by Suleiman I the Magnificent in 1537–1541; the Al-Jazzar Pasha Mosque, Citadel and seawalls of Acre; and the Grand Mahmudi Mosque in Jaffa. Other examples of Ottoman building may be found in Safed.

The story *Of Guns and Mules* begins near the Hassan Bek Mosque, Jaffa, during the opening stages of World War I, the historic event that finally brought this long-lived empire to an end.

CHAPTER ONE
Deportation

I'm lucky, I suppose. Very lucky. And the reason – as these pages will tell you – is that I was able to take part in some of the most important and exciting events that ever happened in Palestine, or *Eretz Israel*, if you want to use the Holy Land's Hebrew name.

But before I get carried away with the excitement of it all, I think I should tell you my story from the very beginning. My name is David – David Levi – and I moved to Palestine with my family a while back, in 1910, to be exact. My father was a trader, "an import-export man," he called himself, and since he wasn't doing too well on New York's Lower East Side, and also because he believed in Zionism, he decided to move his business and his family to Tel Aviv.

This was a brand-new garden city that had recently been established on the Mediterranean coast just north of the old biblical city of Jaffa. Jaffa was mainly an Arab city, while Tel Aviv was Jewish. We – that is, my parents and my younger brother Michael and I – were very happy living there and, despite not seeing certain members of our family or old school friends, we didn't miss New York too much. "After all," Michael used to say, "give me the sun of Tel Aviv over the stickiness of New York any day."

And he was right. We lived in the bright sun, swam in the blue sea just ten minutes away from our house and went to the "Gymnasium Herzliya" school in the center of the city. The school was named after Theodor – or Binyamin Ze'ev, as he is called here – Herzl, the tall, black-bearded Jew from Austria-Hungary. If you remember, he was the man who wrote *The Jewish State*, and said that Jews should make *aliya*, that is, to go and live in Eretz Israel.

I learned to speak Hebrew with my fellow students who came from all over the world – from Russia and Eastern Europe and also from North America. There was even one student who came from Melbourne, Australia. However, it must be said that those of us from English-speaking countries were certainly in the minority.

I also had a girlfriend, Judith, or Yehudit as she preferred to be called. She was as tall as me, had a smooth, olive-colored complexion and soft brown eyes. She had dark brown hair, which she occasionally wore long and loose but she usually braided it for school. I preferred it loose. We both liked wearing pale blue shirts and my friend Nathan said that sometimes we looked like twins, or at least brother and sister. Like me, she was studying in the twelfth grade, but unlike me, she preferred learning English literature. She thought that Shakespeare was the greatest writer in the world and that no one could or would ever beat him. Her favorite play was *Romeo and Juliet* and, one evening after we had seen a performance of it, she couldn't stop crying for an hour. I ask you, is that what's called spending a happy evening?

I must admit, though, I don't mind Shakespeare, but I prefer plays like *Macbeth* where there's more action and the good guys win and the bad ones lose. However, my favorite subject in school was biology. I couldn't think of anything more fascinating than cutting up frogs and mice and studying their insides. When I described the latest experiment we had done in the biology lab, complete with all the gory details, Yehudit went all squeamish and told me to stop.

My parents liked her as well and in an unguarded moment, my mother started talking about a *shidduch* – a marriage match, but I said I was only eighteen. It was much too early to talk about things like that.

Anyway, as I said, I was enjoying life very much when suddenly one morning at the end of 1914, while I was concentrating on my twelfth-grade studies, there was a banging on our front door. When my mother opened it she saw three Turkish policemen standing there. The oldest-looking one, who had fierce eyes and a large black moustache, was holding a long list in his hand. Ignoring my mother, he called for my father. In a short, sharp conversation made up of English, Hebrew and bits of Arabic, he told us that my father and I must leave the house immediately and report to the police station by the port of Jaffa.

"Why?" my father asked.

"No answer," was the gruff reply. "You go now. And him," he said, pointing at me.

"But I have to go to Jerusalem on business," Father said.

"No Jerusalem. No business. Go now."

"My son as well? Are you sure?"

"You David Levi?" he asked, looking at me.

I nodded.

"You eighteen years?"

I nodded again.

He looked at his list. "Yes. You too. Go now."

Father and I just stood there in a state of complete shock; we couldn't move. Mother stood there, her hands over her mouth, her brown eyes wide open. I could see tears were beginning to run down her cheeks. The officer then made a show of unclipping the button on his holster and one of the others loosened the rifle off his shoulder. Father and I still didn't move;

this incident was completely unexpected. We knew that since the war had broken out a few months earlier in August, the Turkish authorities had not been too gentle with the Jewish population in Palestine. This was because they expected us to side with their enemies, the English, the French and the Russians.

"*Tov*, good," my father said and shrugged his shoulders. "I'm sure this is all one big mistake. Come, David, let's go now and sort this out. If we're lucky, I still might be able to get to Jerusalem today."

Accompanied by two Turkish policemen, we were marched off in the direction of the old stone-colored police station. As we made our way along the dusty street, people we knew stopped and waved to us, but quickly disappeared when the policemen made threatening gestures with their rifles.

The police station was a scene of sheer chaos. Friends and acquaintances greeted each other and I saw about ten boys there from my class as well as a dozen from another twelfth-grade class. Over the noise and commotion, I beckoned my friend Nathan Goldstein to come over to where I was standing by the doorway.

"What's happening?" I asked.

"Don't know."

"How long have you been here?"

"Since eight o'clock this morning. And you?"

"I've just arrived with my father. Is your father here as well?"

"Yes, he's over there in the corner talking to Daniel's father."

"Aren't there any girls or women here?" I asked, looking around.

"No, just men and boys of our age. Y'know, twelfth grade. About seventeen or eighteen years old and up."

"Why? Do you think they want us to join their army?"

He shrugged his shoulders. "I don't know, but it's possible."

"Well, I hope not, but legally, I suppose, we are Turkish citizens, aren't we?"

"Yes, but now it seems as if this Turkish Empire's in trouble. The Turks are on the same side as the Germans and so the British, who are fighting the Germans, are also fighting the Turks. Now do you follow?"

I nodded. "But the Brits are much stronger than the Turks, aren't they?"

"That's what they say," Nathan's friend Harold answered.

"I see. But where do we – I mean the Jews in Tel Aviv – fit in with all of this?" I asked.

"Well, David, they see us as possible enemy aliens. You know, like the Christians and the Armenians. If you ask me," Harold continued, "they'll probably stick us in prison to keep us out of the way."

"What! All of us?" I gasped, looking around at the big room, which was now pretty full. I must admit that the idea of going to prison just because I was an enemy alien didn't seem fair. And my very respectable father – him in prison? That really struck me as unbelievable.

But Harold was wrong. The Turks weren't going to stick us in prison to keep us out of the way. They did worse. Later that day, our Turkish guards herded us all together in the courtyard and marched us out in a long column to the port of Jaffa. It was obvious from their faces and their rifles with fixed bayonets that they meant business.

At the port we were organized into long lines, like soldiers on parade, and told to stand still and not move. By now it was very hot and my tongue felt very dry. All I wanted was a drink of water. When I put up my hand, a Turkish soldier shouted and rushed over and hit my hand with the barrel of his rifle. My hand hurt and I stayed thirsty. My father leaned over to me and whispered out of the corner of his mouth, "David, don't ask any questions. Just keep quiet."

Then there were more shouts in Turkish and line by line we were marched up the gangplank onto a waiting steamer, whose vibrations let us know the engines were running. We were pushed up onto the crowded upper decks but I was actually relieved that we hadn't been forced to go below.

"Where do you think they're taking us?" I asked my father, who had now taken off his dark jacket and waistcoat. He was wiping his forehead with what had once been a clean white handkerchief.

"I don't know, son. Maybe to Constantinople."

"You mean to join the Turkish army?"

"Yes, or to some sort of internment camp. But if they want to make soldiers out of us, they'd have a hard job with me, don't you think?"

"Yes, Father," I agreed, half-smiling. It was hard to imagine my short, pale-faced father in a uniform carrying a rifle and pack, let alone actually fighting the enemy.

But my father was wrong on two counts. We weren't being taken to Constantinople, and we weren't going to be turned into Turkish soldiers. Nathan as usual came up with the correct answer.

"David," he said, as he pushed his way past a few men to reach me at the rails where I was standing, "I've just heard. We're going to Egypt!"

"Egypt? Why there?"

"Well, for the Turks it gets us out of Tel Aviv or Palestine or wherever, and Egypt is nearer than Turkey. So that makes it easier for them to ship us out, to get rid of us, no?"

And then it struck me that the Turks, who were usually not very well organized, had gotten themselves organized properly for this deportation, as it was called. An hour or so later the vibrations on the steamer grew louder, as did the shouts of the sailors on board to the men on the quay below. Within minutes, after various ropes had been untied and cast aside, our ship with its load of some seven hundred Jews sailed out of the ancient port of Jaffa, on our way westward to Egypt.

Naturally we all crowded to the sides of the boat to take our last look at Eretz Israel. I focused on some of the buildings I knew, and I'm sure, like everyone else, I wondered when we'd be coming home again. I must admit that I had a few tears in my eyes, but when I saw Nathan looking at me, I quickly wiped them and cracked a stupid joke about going on holiday, paid for by Hassan Bey, the Turkish extremist who hated all "nonbelievers."

"Nathan," I asked, pointing at the far end of the ship, "didn't Mr. Silberstein and his two sons apply for Turkish citizenship? I mean, that's what Jonathan told me in school."

"Yes, he told me that as well. But the Turks tied them up in so much red tape that they never got it. And that's true for lots of other people as well, or so I've heard."

"So here they are with us as enemy aliens."

"That's right. Our neighbors are enemy aliens."

"By the way," I asked, "is there any way I can let Yehudit know I'm here? And does your family know you're here?"

"I hope so. I wrote a note and passed it to someone while we were being marched off to the police station."

"I saw my father do the same, that is, after you told us about Egypt. He threw it overboard to someone on the quayside. But it's still going to be a terrible shock when my family and Yehudit find out what's happened to us."

"Well, my friend, there's nothing we can do about that, is there? So let's not think about it for the moment and see if we can find something to eat. I'm starving."

This time I was faster than Nathan at finding food and I found a Turkish crewman who was selling sandwiches and hot sweet tea. It wasn't very filling but it was better than nothing, and now all I hoped was that Yehudit would hear about what had happened to me and that I wouldn't be seasick. Fortunately I wasn't. The three-hundred-mile journey to Alexandria was uneventful, and even pleasant in a way. That is, if I didn't think about why it was happening and what would happen to us once we got to Egypt.

Later I heard that soon after we had been deported, life at home grew worse by the day. The Turkish governor Jemal Pasha, helped by the cruel Hassan Bey, started throwing the Jews who remained in Tel Aviv into jail, or exiling them to Tiberias in the far north. The Turks also banned all sorts of Jewish organizations and unions. Jewish defense units, such as *Hashomer*, were broken up and their weapons were confiscated. The Turks also arrested some important members of the *Yishuv*, the Jewish community, such as David Ben-Gurion and Yitzhak Ben-Zvi, simply because they were the editors of a Zionist newspaper.

Sometime on the journey I must have fallen asleep, because the next thing I remember was my father tapping me on my shoulder.

"Wake up, son. We're here."

"Where?" I asked, stretching my arms and rubbing my eyes.

"Alexandria. But I've heard we're not staying here."

"Why? Where are we going?"

"Somewhere near Cairo, but I don't know what it's called."

"That's good," I said. "It's nearer home."

"True, but not much. But if you think you're going to do a Moses and walk over the Sinai Desert to the Promised Land, you're very much mistaken. Home is hundreds of miles away, and if the desert doesn't kill you, the Bedouin will."

"So, Father, maybe we could steal a boat and try and get back home that way?"

"Maybe. But we'll talk about that later." This meant that we wouldn't.

But I couldn't stop thinking about home. "Father," I asked. "What do you think is going to happen to Mother and Michael? Who is going to look after them? What are they going to do for money? Mother has never had to work – what will she do?"

"I don't know, David. Money shouldn't be an immediate problem – I have been doing quite well recently – but if we're going to be away for a long time, then your mother will have to start thinking of what to do."

"Maybe Michael will be able to get some sort of work, you know, after school."

"Perhaps," he said thoughtfully, and then he stared out at the water for a long time before he spoke again. "David, try not to let these thoughts worry you. There's not much we can do about it now. All we can hope is that this whole thing has turned out to be one big mistake and they'll be sending us back soon."

"I hope you're right, otherwise we'll have to try to escape, despite what you said before."

But for the moment, if the truth be told, I was too sticky, too hungry and too dirty to really think about escaping even though all I wanted was Yehudit, my own bed back in Tel Aviv and a good long soak in a hot bath. However, I was sure I wouldn't be getting any of these things soon. Shortly afterwards we were taken off the ship and escorted to a rather primitive-looking train that was waiting for us by the quayside.

"Does anyone know where we're going?" I asked in a loud voice.

"Don't know" and shrugs of the shoulder were the only answers I got as I looked out at the light brown, sandy scenery. I dozed off again. I don't know how much time passed before I was again woken up by my father.

"Wake up, David. We're here."

"Where's here?"

"Gabbari."

"Gabbari. Where's that?"

"Somewhere not too far from Cairo. Some sort of suburb, I believe. But look, there's an army camp over there. Can you see the rows of tents?"

I stood up and looked out the grubby window. It was true. There, not far from the railway tracks, were rows and rows of khaki-colored army tents. But the strange thing was that in the middle of them stood a flag pole, and the flag flying at the top was none other than the red, white and blue Union Jack, the flag of Great Britain.

"Father! Look, it's a British army camp! Not a Turkish or Egyptian one. Look at the flag!"

I was right. There in a sandy and dusty plain, a few miles outside Cairo, the British army had set up this camp for deportees and it was here at Gabbari that I was to make some of the most important decisions of my life.

CHAPTER TWO
The Zion Mule Corps

In a roped-off corner of the British military camp at Gabbari, Egypt, an important meeting was being held. There, in a large, sand-colored bell-tent marked "Officers and Admin. Staff only," several officers were sitting around a table, a large map of the Middle East spread out in front of them.

The most senior officer present was Lieutenant Colonel John Henry Patterson. As well as being the author of *The Man-Eaters of Tsavo* and *In the Grip of the Nyika*, two exciting books that had recorded his adventures in Africa, this career officer had served in the British army for many years. He had served with distinction in the South African Boer War (1899–1902) and had rapidly been promoted through the ranks. Patterson, born in Ireland, was a Protestant, and he loved the Bible and the biblical Land of Israel with a great passion.

It was now, as an experienced officer, that he saw his next task – the setting up of a unit of Jewish soldiers within the framework of the British army – as a labor of love.

To do so he was to be helped by Captain Joseph Trumpeldor, an honorary captain who would help him organize the future ZMC, the Zion Mule Corps. The Russian-born Trumpeldor sat opposite Patterson, while next to him sat another Russian-born officer, Vladimir – now called Ze'ev – Jabotinsky.

"Gentlemen," Patterson began, looking at the two men while pouring himself a glass of water. "The reason I've called you here today is to discuss the formation and establishment of a Jewish military unit, here in Egypt. The aim of this unit will be to help the British army in the Middle East, that is, to fight and beat the Turks and their German supporters.

"As you may know, General Maxwell has appointed me to be the commanding officer of this unit and, as such, I've already been in contact with the Jewish leaders in Cairo and Alexandria. They in turn have promised me that they will do all in their power to help me establish such a unit. This means that they will encourage as many men as possible to volunteer to join the ZMC, and that while some of the men will come from the local Egyptian Jewish community, others will come from the hundreds of Jews who have recently been deported to these shores by the Turks from Palestine."

"However," Patterson continued, looking at Trumpeldor and Jabotinsky, "before we go any further with this, we have two major problems to solve. One: is this unit to be an active fighting one or not? And two: are these men to be used only to kick Johnny Turk out of the Holy Land, or are they to be an integral part of the British army and so take part in whatever the army is asked to do here in the Middle East, as well as in France and the Western Front?"

He sat back and looked at the two men. Jabotinsky started cleaning his glasses as he searched for a suitable answer, while Trumpeldor looked out the window of the tent into the distance and said nothing.

Seeing that he was not going to get an immediate reply to his questions, Patterson decided to change his tactics. "Gentlemen," he said, "before you give me your answers, please tell me something about yourselves. All I know about you is from a few notes that the administration people have given me. I know from your records that you were both born in Russia: you, Lieutenant Jabotinsky, were born in Odessa, and you,

Captain Trumpeldor, are from, where was it? Ah, yes, here it is, Pyatigorsk in Caucasia. Am I right?"

Both men nodded in agreement.

"Then I suggest you start." The colonel pointed to Jabotinsky.

Jabotinsky put his thin-framed glasses back on his nose and, looking like a school teacher, started to stand up.

"No, no. You may remain seated. This is an informal meeting, even though it may turn out to be very important. So Lieutenant Jabotinsky, please begin."

Jabotinsky pulled himself up in his chair, coughed and cleared his throat.

"Well, sir," he said in a thin voice, "I was born Vladimir Jabotinsky in Russia, as you know, but I prefer using my Hebrew name, Ze'ev."

"Doesn't Ze'ev mean wolf in Hebrew?" Patterson asked.

"Yes, sir."

"Please continue. I'll try not to interrupt you anymore."

"Yes, sir. Well, after I finished school in Russia, where fortunately I was good at languages..."

"Yes, I can see that," said Patterson, forgetting his promise not to interrupt.

"Then at the age of eighteen I became the editor of a newspaper in Odessa and I wrote under the pen name of Altalena. In 1903 I started to become involved in fighting for the rights of the Jews in Russia and then later I moved to Italy and Austria where I studied law. I continued with my newspaper career and became even more involved in the Zionist movement, you know, the movement for resettling the Jewish nation in their ancient homeland."

"Yes, I've read about the Zionist movement," Patterson said. "Please continue."

"Well, sir, when this war broke out in 1914, I saw it as the golden opportunity to throw the Turks out of our country, and that is, sir, as you British would say, my life in a nutshell."

"I see," said Patterson, leaning forward. "So you haven't really had much experience of army life, have you?"

"No, sir. Not in the British army and not in the Russian one either. But my friend here, Captain Trumpeldor, has."

Patterson turned to Trumpeldor, who had been sitting there silently, studying the map in front of him. "Right, Captain. It's your turn now."

Trumpeldor pushed the map aside and started talking. His Russian accent was thicker than Jabotinsky's but his English was clearly understandable.

"Like my fellow British soldier from Russia here," Trumpeldor began, casting a smile at Jabotinsky, "I was born at the beginning of the 1880s but, unlike him, I served in the Russian army for several years. In fact I gave up my dental studies in order to volunteer and serve in the czar's army. And that, sir, is where I lost my left arm. In the Russo-Japanese War, fighting at Port Arthur ten years ago. I lost it during the siege that went on for eleven months, that is, before spending a few months in a Japanese prisoner-of-war camp. Yes, sir. I suppose that I was just like my father. He also served in the czar's army for many years."

"But tell me, Captain, wasn't that somewhat rare – I mean, for a Jew to serve in the Russian army?"

"No, not especially, sir. The Russian authorities called up many young Jews, sir. They hoped that if they kept those Jews in the army for long enough, they would forget their Judaism. But fortunately, that didn't happen to me. But what was rare, if I may say so, was for a Jew like me to be promoted to become an officer and also to be decorated for bravery, sir."

"Yes, Captain. I'd heard about that. I heard that you had been awarded the Russian equivalent of our Victoria Cross, is that right?"

"Yes, sir, but I'd rather not talk about that."

"I understand. And then you came to Palestine, right?"

"Yes, sir. I came here two years ago and joined a group of *halutzim*, er, pioneers, sir, who were setting up a communal settlement, a *kibbutz* we call it. It was on the shore of the *Kinneret*, the Sea of Galilee. We call it Degania, which is Hebrew for cornflower. And then the Turks called me up to serve in their army but I refused. So with hundreds of other Jews, they deported me and I ended up here."

"Thank you, Captain. And now," Patterson said, facing the two officers, "I understand that both of you have already discussed the question of setting up a unit of Jewish soldiers who will fight together with the British army. Am I right?"

"Yes, sir."

"And what are your conclusions?"

"Well, sir," Jabotinsky began. "Here, my friend Captain Trumpeldor and myself have different opinions. We both believe that if Jewish soldiers fight with the British army, we'll have a better chance of getting rid of the Turks and gaining our own independence. But," and here Jabotinsky paused for a moment as if to stress their different points of view, "Captain Trumpeldor here is prepared to be more, er…how shall I say it, er…more generous than me."

"What do you mean, generous?" Patterson looked puzzled.

"Sir, Captain Trumpeldor believes that the Jews should be willing to take on almost any task that the British army wants, at least in the Middle East, whereas I believe that the Jewish soldiers should be used by the British only to get rid of the

Turks in Palestine. That is, we take part in the fighting only in Palestine, sir."

"With Great Britain taking over afterwards?" the colonel asked quietly.

"Maybe, sir. I'm not sure about that one yet," Jabotinsky replied, looking at Trumpeldor. "You see, sir, a resolution was passed at a meeting of the Palestine Refugees' Committee and, if I may quote it, they talked about the formation of a Jewish Legion which would be used in Palestine. This means, of course, that we will have to throw out the Turks, to finish off the Ottoman occupation of my country. As you know, Colonel, they've been there for four hundred years and..."

"Yes, I know all that," Patterson interrupted, thinking that the bespectacled Jabotinsky was beginning to sound like his history teacher from his own school days back in Ireland. "And you, Captain, don't agree with this, right?"

"No, sir. I don't. I believe that it is in our interest – the Jewish people, that is – to earn the respect of Britain as the major power in the Middle East. To do so, we should help in the war effort and cooperate with the British in any way we can."

Jabotinsky was shaking his head. Patterson continued.

"Even as a service corps, Captain? I mean not actually being involved in the fighting?"

"Yes, sir, although, like my friend here, I would prefer to be actually involved in the fighting, as you call it. To take part in the action, and not just be seen as hanging on to the coattails of the British army, sir."

"I see. And what about fighting only in the Holy Land, in Palestine, as Lieutenant Jabotinsky here has just mentioned?"

"Sir, I think it would be better if we did our bit in the Holy Land, that is getting rid of the Turks there, but if the British army thinks otherwise, then so be it."

At this, Jabotinsky scowled a bit and coughed, but had the good grace not to say anything. He did not want to make a bad impression on an officer who, in all probability, could end up as his own commanding officer.

That night, the three officers had another meeting in the same tent, together with General John Maxwell, the commanding officer of the British forces in Egypt. At the end of an hour's discussion, Jabotinsky felt very disappointed as the general stood up to leave.

"I'm very sorry, gentlemen," Maxwell said, "but I refuse to consider the separate formation of a unit of Jewish soldiers fighting within the framework of the British army. And I certainly don't believe that such a unit," and here he looked straight at Jabotinsky, "that such a unit should only take a part in the hostilities in Palestine." He then turned to Colonel Patterson, who was sitting next to Trumpeldor. "However, if the Jews want to fight as a separate unit, and are prepared to be an auxiliary unit – a service corps – then I'm sure the British army will be happy to use their services in a unit like the transport corps, or something like that. In fact, such a unit would be a great help to us when we start moving things in the Middle East."

"At Gallipoli? By the Dardanelles?" Trumpeldor asked, reflecting parade-ground rumors.

"Maybe, Captain, but I'm not at liberty at the moment to give you any more details. However, I promise I will tell you more if you agree to join us. So, good night, gentlemen. No doubt we'll meet again later." And he pushed open the tent flap and walked out into the clear air of the Egyptian night.

That night Trumpeldor and Jabotinsky had a long and drawn-out argument about the wisdom of raising a unit of Jewish troops, and if so, how much it should become involved with the British army. The same points were repeated time and again, and it was only as the sun was beginning to rise that the two men worked out a compromise. Jabotinsky would continue with his political fight on behalf of an independent Jewish state in Palestine, while Trumpeldor would become Colonel Patterson's second-in-command of the Zion Mule Corps, the ZMC. In this way, Trumpeldor would act as the link between the ordinary Jewish soldiers and the higher ranks of the British army. They hoped that the new unit would be fighting in the Middle East and would in the end be responsible for ending the Ottoman Empire's four-hundred-year rule over Eretz Israel.

All that Trumpeldor and Jabotinsky needed now was to be able to persuade the hundreds of Jewish refugees from Palestine as well as the local Egyptian Jews to join them. To do so, they would have to arrange meetings with all of these would-be soldiers and persuade them that the best thing they could do was to join the British army.

CHAPTER THREE
David Levi, ZMC

A few days after arriving in Gabbari, Nathan pushed the tent flaps open and called me.

"David, David! Get up! Come with me. There's going to be an important meeting in the big tent."

"What about?"

"About setting up a Jewish unit in the British army. At least that's what everyone says."

"Why?"

"To fight the Turks, you idiot. To kick 'em out of Eretz Israel."

"Sounds like a good idea. Wait a minute, will you? I'm coming." And leaving a trail of dust behind us we both ran over to the large white tent in the middle of the camp.

The huge reception tent had already been prepared for a meeting, and when we arrived, we found over two hundred men sitting on wooden benches facing the far end. There were many empty spaces at the back, but we pushed our way toward the front and found a couple of places to sit in the third row. There was a noisy atmosphere of excitement and expectation. It seemed as though everyone was turning to his neighbor and asking if what they had heard was true.

"Do they really want to organize a Jewish battalion?"

"Are we all going to be called up?"

"Will we be fighting back home or on the Western Front?"

"Who's going to be in charge?"

"Do you think we'll have our own badges and things like that?"

Suddenly all the noise died down as a British officer entered the reception tent from the side and took his place behind the long folding table at the front.

"Look, he's a colonel. At least I think so. Look at the pip and crown on his shoulder."

"The pip?"

"Yes, that star below the crown. Don't you know anything?"

The lieutenant colonel, for that is what he was, sat down and faced the expectant men. He did not say anything. Like Mr. Wasserman, our strict chemistry teacher, he ignored the noise and the chatter, which died down immediately. He just kept looking around, as if he were judging the men sitting in rows facing him. A few moments later, a couple of other officers joined him and one of them sat down next to the lieutenant colonel while the other unrolled a large map of Turkey and the Middle East and hung it on a nail before sitting down.

"I wonder what they want," I whispered to Nathan.

"Well, keep quiet and we'll find out soon."

"Nathan, do you know who those men are?" I asked, pointing to the front.

"No, but I think one of them is called Trumpinsky, or something like that."

I looked around. By now the tent was full and men were even standing around at the outer edges. Then one of the officers at the top table stood up.

"Will you men at the sides, yes, you over there, please open all the flaps, or we'll all suffocate in here?"

A few moments later he stood up again and held up his hand as a sign for silence. I could feel the renewed hum of whispered conversations die away, and within a minute the tent was silent. Only the buzz of flies and the sound of men quietly slapping themselves or wiping the pesky flies off their faces could be heard. Then the colonel stood up. He was tall and slim and his smart khaki British army uniform seemed to complement his brown hair and mustache. In contrast to us, in our civilian clothing, he looked every inch a British officer, as did the other two sitting next to him. It was obvious from the way he stood and held himself that he was used to being a commanding officer. Men listened to him.

"Good morning. I am Lieutenant Colonel Patterson, and I have called you here because it is my task to ask for volunteers for the establishment of a transport unit which will operate within the framework of the British army, here in the Middle East."

He half-turned and pointed to Egypt and the Ottoman Empire on the map hanging behind him.

"Yes, we know where that is," Nathan whispered to me. "We've lived there."

"The aim of this new unit," Patterson continued, in his crisp Irish-accented English, "will be to aid the British units serving our main effort in this part of the world, which, as you may know, is to drive the Turks out of the Middle East – and that of course includes the Holy Land, where many of you come from."

I looked around and noticed many heads nodding.

"Gentlemen and future volunteers," Patterson said, "I am not at liberty as yet to tell you what plans His Majesty's government has for this part of the world and how they are to be executed, but please rest assured that when the time comes, those of you who volunteer will feel that they have committed themselves to a very worthy endeavor.

"That is the general gist of what I have to tell you at the present moment. If any of you have any questions, please raise your hands and Captain Trumpeldor, here on my right, will answer them."

He then took his briefcase and stepped smartly out of the tent. Many hands started waving in the air and the buzz of conversation and questions started again.

"Will we be getting uniforms?"

"Is the British army going to pay us, or will we be unpaid volunteers?"

"Will our officers be English or Jewish?"

"What will our unit be called?"

"Will all the Jews serve together or will we be spread out among other units?"

"What about training?"

"And guns? I've never fired one in my life."

"Are we going to stay here in Egypt?"

"…or be sent to Constantinople?"

"…or Jerusalem?"

"Will our rations be kosher?"

"Vill ve only haf to spik English?" a heavily bearded man with a foreign accent behind me asked.

The question and answer period lasted for over half an hour and at the end Captain Trumpeldor raised a handful of papers as a sign that he wanted silence. It took a couple of minutes for everyone to settle down, but the atmosphere was still charged.

However, it seemed that even after all this there were still a number of cynical men who thought that the British army were out to exploit us. Some of them talked about "cannon fodder," while others thought that the British army just wanted us to do their dirty work for them.

"Just you see how they use those men who are not English on the Western Front," someone said. "They do all the digging and *schlepping* of the heavy equipment."

"That's right," his friend added. "Or we'll end up like those Egyptian work brigades. You know, those poor buggers here in Cairo and Alexandria who do all the cleaning up in the British army camps. They might do a good job, but they aren't thought of as soldiers. They're just seen as local civilians in the British army. No privileges or perks, nothing. You mark my words. That's what that lot wants from us," he said, jerking his thumb in the direction where the British officers were sitting.

But before anyone could mark his words, an officer on the right of Captain Trumpeldor stood up and the tent was silent again.

"I want you men to see me, or rather us," and he held out his arm to include all the men at the head table, "as representatives of the people of England. And as such, we are appealing to you, the Jewish people, in the name of friendship, a friendship which will surely continue within a Jewish country of Palestine. Can you now turn down this outstretched arm which is calling for your support?"

There was a moment's silence as he stood there hoping his words had hit home. They had. Suddenly a happy chaos broke out and we were all clapping and smiling as he sat down.

It took Trumpeldor a few minutes to obtain silence once again.

"Right," Trumpeldor started, in his Russian-flavored English. "Now that that is settled and I have finished answering your questions, I will leave this pile of forms on the table by the entrance over there. Those who wish to volunteer, please fill in all the necessary details. Please write very clearly in pen, and in English. Thank you."

"But I can't write in English," someone called out. "I know only Hebrew and Yiddish."

"I'll help you," another voice called out.

Despite the good-natured noise and the pushing, we managed to form a long line in front of the table and each of us in turn took a form headed "B.2505A. Short Service. (For the Duration of the War.)," and returned to our benches to fill them in.

"What's this 'ZMC' here?" I asked Nathan, pointing to a circular symbol at the top of the page.

"Don't know. It's probably the name of this unit, I guess. Anyway, enough questions. Let's just fill them in."

The forms asked for the usual details: Name? Address? Are you a British subject? Age? Trade? Married? We finished filling them in, signed and dated them and put them in the cardboard box by the entrance to the reception tent. As I walked out of the stuffy tent and into the glare of the Egyptian desert, I noticed the British officer, the one who had been sitting at the table with Colonel Patterson and Captain Trumpeldor, looking very pleased at the growing pile of forms. It looked as though everyone there had filled one in and the cardboard box was overflowing.

Later, I heard that on that day, over six hundred men had volunteered to join the ZMC, the Zion Mule Corps, but little did we know what we were volunteering for. By signing that form and putting it in that box, little did I guess what my future contribution to the history of the Land of Israel would be, and little did I guess how long I would be a soldier in the service of King George the Fifth.

Badge of the ZMC Mule Corps

CHAPTER FOUR
To Cape Helles

The swearing-in ceremony for the Zion Mule Corps took place on April 1, 1915.

"Do you think it's a coincidence that it's April Fool's Day today?" Nathan whispered as we stood in line. We were assembled in a large open square formation, three sides of which consisted of the new volunteers to the British army, such as Nathan, me and our new friend, Jacob Marks. The fourth side consisted of various British army officers such as Lieutenant Colonel Patterson, General Maxwell, Captain Trumpeldor and Lieutenant Jabotinsky, even though he didn't think that the future Zion Mule Corps would do anything much for the Jewish cause. In fact, he looked more like a schoolmaster in army uniform rather than an army officer serving with His Majesty's Forces in the Middle East.

Even though this parade probably meant nothing special to most of the British officers present, it made me very proud to be one of the nearly seven hundred Jewish volunteers who were now wearing a British army uniform with a Star of David badge sewn on to it.

"Nathan," I whispered out of the side of my mouth, as a sergeant was standing in front of us. "Do you realize that we are probably serving in the first Jewish army since Judah Hamaccabi fought the Greeks nearly two thousand years ago? I wish my family and Yehudit could see me now. They'd be so proud to see me in my uniform."

Nathan nodded and put a finger on his lips. "Shhhh! General Maxwell is going to say something."

The general then urged his gleaming black stallion forward a few paces and waited for silence. In fact, everything about the general was polished and gleaming – his badges of rank, his Sam Browne belt, the trappings on his horse, everything. He looked most impressive, every inch a commander of men.

In a loud and clear voice he told us that the eyes of the Jewish people would be on us, the new Zion Mule Corps. He said that despite the fact that we had been called up to serve as a service unit, we should not feel lowly, even though we were to work with mules, and not with rifles and bayonets. We should feel proud to be taking our part in the British army, an army that had fought against Napoleon, against corrupt rulers in India, and had recently beaten the Boers in South Africa.

"And let me quote to you from one of our greatest English poets, John Milton. Did he not say, 'They also serve who only stand and wait'? And so I say to you, you the men of the Hebrew nation, you will do more than just stand and wait. You too will become an integral part of this army, this force which will defeat the Turk, and free this area, the Middle East, from the yoke of the Ottoman Empire after four hundred years."

Several men burst into applause before a sharp look from Lieutenant Colonel Patterson stopped them, but I did notice that General Maxwell smiled a little as he moved his horse back into the side of the square. Our commanding officer then moved his chestnut horse forward to take over from where his superior officer had just stood. Like the general, Lieutenant Colonel Patterson had a gleaming uniform and horse. He then sat up even straighter, if that were possible, in his saddle and went on to tell us that all of the officers present on this day – apart from a few experienced men who had volunteered to serve with him – were new to the military. We were to have full respect at all times for all of our officers, even though some of them, like us, had not yet in fact experienced a real battle.

"The organization of this new unit, the Zion Mule Corps, is to be as follows," Patterson announced. "It will be divided into two separate but parallel units, one consisting of English troops and the other of Jewish troops from Palestine and Egypt. Both units will have Anglo-Indian lieutenants as their officers and they, in turn, will be responsible for four companies. These commanding officers will be aided by adjutants, second lieutenants and various NCOs who have come from Palestine."

"What's an NCO?" someone whispered behind me.

"Non-commissioned officer," his friend answered. "Now shhhh. I'm trying to listen."

"And these NCOs," Patterson continued, "will be drawn from the Jewish volunteers. Furthermore, each company will be divided into four platoons which, in turn, will be divided into four sections. Other officers and men will include specialists with horses and mules, as well as blacksmiths, saddlers, medical and veterinary staff. That will be all for now. And so, to conclude this parade, we will run up the new flag of the corps, the Zion Mule Corps, and sing the National Anthem and then dismiss."

And as he said this, the Union Jack was run up one flagpole and, while the light breeze unfurled it, the new flag of our new Zion Mule Corps was run up on the other. I must admit that I felt very proud to see the circular symbol with the *Magen David* in the middle flying proudly over our camp. I wiped a tear from my eye and noticed that several other men were doing the same, including Nathan, who was pretending that he wasn't.

Following a drumroll, we sang "God Save the King," turned sharply on our heels and made our way back to the long lines of tents behind us.

"So that's it," I said to Nathan and Jacob, as we sat down on our army cots. "The ZMC really exists now. A Jewish fighting force."

"You might be right there, David, but what are they going to do with us? Make us their 'hewers of wood and drawers of water,' as the Bible says?"

"I hope not," I replied. "I didn't volunteer just to carry pails of water around for thirsty horses…"

"Mules," Jacob corrected me.

"Well, whatever happens, I want to see some action."

"Well, my friend, you'll just have to wait for your action. First of all, you'll have to learn how to march in step and how to use a rifle. Shouting 'bang! bang!' at the enemy won't get you very far."

Nathan was right, of course. I may have wanted to see some action but, if the truth were told, all I was at the moment was a civilian, a civvy in uniform.

First of all, we had to undergo some training. I had to learn how to use a gun or, as I was to call it from now on, a rifle. Some of the men were issued – the army did not say "given" – rifles that had been captured from the Turks, but I was issued a British short-muzzled Lee-Enfield rifle. They told me that it fired .303 bullets and it weighed over eight and a half pounds – without the bayonet, which weighed about another pound. The rifle was about four feet long without a bayonet and just over five feet with one. Its muzzle velocity (whatever that meant) was 2440 feet per second.

"That means," Jacob said one day, after we had finished our first day at the firing range, "that you mustn't stand in front of it – that is, where the little hole is."

"Very funny," I said, rubbing my hand, where the sharp edge of an entrenching tool had taken the skin off the top end of my finger.

The entrenching tool, which at first I called a spade, was part of the gear I had been issued, along with a water bottle, a knife, fork and spoon, spare socks, a shaving kit, shirts and underwear, a greatcoat, groundsheet and a first-aid kit as well as wire cutters, ammunition pouches, a thick webbing belt and, of course, my uniform. As part of the uniform, I received a flat cap, although later this would be exchanged for a tin helmet. All of my gear had to be packed – or rather, crammed – into a large backpack and a small side pack, which was also known as a haversack.

I must admit that, although I may have looked like a soldier in the photograph that someone took of me to send home to my family in Tel Aviv, I felt more like a pack mule, the ones that later we would be responsible for. When I marched on parade, my new boots squeaked, and moving about in my new uniform and packs was certainly not very comfortable.

However, life wasn't really as bad as all that. I didn't need to wear or carry all my gear about all the time; I could leave things such as spare clothes, shaving kit and the heavy khaki greatcoat behind in my tent. But that caused a problem as there were always soldiers who lost things, and they would "borrow" yours to save themselves from getting into trouble during the regular kit inspections. I learned to mark my things very clearly and so usually I did not have too many problems on that score. And of course, "When in Rome, do as the Romans do." So whenever any of my stuff went missing, especially just before an inspection or parade, then I had no alternative other than to "borrow" from someone else!

I enjoyed being on the rifle range. As time progressed, my shooting improved and one day I even scored four bull's-eyes! One of our training officers asked me if I wanted to be a sniper, but I turned the offer down. I wanted to stay with the ZMC.

"Even though you'll be in a service unit?" he asked.

"Yes, sir. All my friends are in the Mule Corps and, if you don't mind, sir, I would prefer to stay in a Jewish unit, even though it is a service one."

He walked off, scratching his head and muttering something about some people who don't realize when they're being offered a good deal.

And so our training continued. We had lectures on military topics; weapons training with rifles, pistols and bayonets; long-distance marches wearing full pack; and first-aid courses. In addition, we had to do our fair (or unfair!) share of duties in the camp kitchens.

Sometimes, it must be admitted, this was good, as it was a way to grab some extra food, but sometimes it was nearly as tough as – and definitely more boring than – our training exercises. This was especially so when we had to clean the really huge, dirty and sticky army cooking pots called dixies. The worst part of this was when the cooks had burned the potatoes, semolina, rice or whatever; then cleaning these dixies took over twice as long as it normally did. The cleaned pots would be inspected and, if we hadn't cleaned them properly, we would have to clean them again. Fortunately, this happened only once to me.

"When you get married," Nathan quipped one day when I was scouring a burnt dixie particularly violently, "your Yehudit will be impressed to see how you wash dishes and dixies."

However, you shouldn't think that our training period consisted only of hard work. Every so often we would be allowed time off and then we would go into Cairo or go sightseeing. The first thing I did once I was in Cairo was to join an organized trip to see the Sphinx and the pyramids at Giza. I found out that the Sphinx at Giza was not the only one but it was the oldest. It was huge. Later I read that it was almost 190 feet long and that the lion-like head alone was thirty feet long and fourteen feet wide, the whole structure being almost seventy feet high.

Of course, going to Cairo for a night out was great fun as well, although of a different sort. We saw all sorts of people there, including soldiers from other countries who were also fighting the Turks and Germans. The noisiest and the pushiest were the Anzacs, the soldiers from the Australian and New Zealand Army Corps. They were usually more tanned and brawny than the British and French soldiers, and had a reputation for drinking and brawling, often just for its own sake. They seemed to enjoy making fun of the British officers, and although the Anzacs were supposed to salute them, they never did. Or, if they did, their salute was a mockery of the real thing, and often done while they tried to mimic the upper-class British accents. The Brits would usually look embarrassed and try to ignore the whole thing.

But one evening, all this – the training and the days off – came to an end. I found Nathan and Jacob sitting on their camp beds writing letters home.

"Aren't you going to write to Yehudit?" Nathan asked.

"No," I replied. "I wrote her a couple of pages before we went on kitchen duty. And I also wrote home. I'm worried about my mother and brother. I haven't heard anything from them since we arrived here." Then I asked Jacob, who usually knew what was going on, what he knew about Gallipoli, a place I'd overheard several officers talk about in a serious way.

"Gallipoli?" asked Jacob, looking up. "Oh, that's where the Brits tried to break through the Turkish barricade across the Dardanelles."

"And failed," Nathan added.

"Yes. And I've heard that they're planning to send us, the Mule Corps, out there to help the British army and support them when they land. In fact, someone told me that since the Brits hadn't succeeded in breaking through the blockade by sea, they were going to try it overland."

"What?" I asked. "Are we going to be a part of that?"

Jacob nodded. "At least that's what I've heard. The good life here is over for us and, as far as I know, it's Gallipoli, here we come. Helping the Brits to fight the Turks."

"But what's that got to do with the ZMC and trying to get the Turks out of Eretz Israel?" I asked.

"Nothing directly," Jacob said. "But if we can help weaken the Turks' hold in this part of the Middle East, then they'll be forced to leave Palestine. Isn't that true, Nathan?"

"Well, they say that's what Captain Trumpeldor believes, even though Jabotinsky doesn't."

We soon found out that, whatever Jabotinsky thought about the Mule Corps and our fighting with the British, it was too late to change anything. Soon after, over 550 of us were loaded onto trucks and taken down to the port. There we were kept busy throughout the following day and night loading up the transport ships with all the equipment we would need. In addition to the guns and ammunition, the tents and shovels, baggage and forage, we had to load the horses and mules aboard. This was done by wrapping slings around them, under their bellies, and then hoisting them aboard. The animals did not like this and showed it by kicking and making all sorts of horrible noises. Eventually, however, we got them all aboard where we tied them down in their stalls and gave them something to eat in an attempt to calm them down. Since one of our main duties at Gallipoli would be to supply the troops with water, we also had to pack thousands of metal water containers which would be carried in special wooden frames strapped to the backs of the mules. Of course, hundreds of these frames had to be carried aboard as well.

It was only after we had finished all this exhausting work, and after a short parade on the dockside, that we, ourselves, marched up the gangplanks of His Majesty's transport ships, the *Hymettus* and the *Anglo-Egyptian*. On April 17, 1915, we set sail for Cape Helles, the southernmost point of the Gallipoli peninsula. Fortunately, just before leaving, I was able to see my father for half an hour; his last action was to bless me and wish me good luck in my new life. "If you and the ZMC manage to rid us of the Turks, it will all have been worth it," he said, trying to hold back his tears. I would remember these parting words many times over the next three years.

The 750-mile journey from Egypt to Gallipoli, across the Mediterranean from south to north, passed uneventfully, although a Turkish torpedo boat was in the area and threatened to sink us. Apart from that, the only other unpleasant thing was that Nathan and several others became seasick as we passed the island of Crete.

"It's not fair," Nathan said, retching over the side. "This didn't happen to me when we sailed from Tel Aviv to Egypt. Now look at me."

His normally suntanned face was a pale greenish color and I could not help laughing. He tried to look serious, but failed.

"Look, I've survived the British army's food. I've survived eating *pita* and *humus* in the *shuk*, the market in Cairo, and I even survived that terrible camel ride when we went on that trip to see the Sphinx. Now, here in the middle of the Mediterranean Sea, I'm as sick as a dog. There's simply no justice in this world." And he leaned over the side once again.

I agreed with him and gave him some water to rinse out his mouth. "Don't worry," I said. "I'm sure that once the action starts, you'll forget all about your guts."

I was right, but I wasn't pleased about the action that greeted us as we approached the landing beaches at Cape Helles. Just as we were moving in to the shore, there were several bright flashes of light and tremendously loud thunderclaps that rang in my ears. Suddenly I felt bits of hot jagged metal falling on us like rain. Something was burning the back of my hand and I saw a black and bloody red mark where a piece of shrapnel had landed on me. I could smell burning flesh. Mine! Men were shouting and running all over the place. The Turkish troops on the cliff tops overlooking the beaches had seen us approach and had fired some artillery shells which had exploded, showering us with burning hot pieces of shrapnel.

The yelling, screaming and chaos continued. Officers shouted out orders, but each man was looking out for himself, hoping to find some sort of shelter from this burning, lethal rain. There were cries of pain and cries for medics, and for the first time in my life I saw men seriously wounded as blood, burnt flesh and uniforms all came together in a deadly mixture. The ship's captain had switched off all the lights, so that we would not present so clear a target for the Turkish gunners, but the darkness on the deck just added to the hellish confusion. The noise that rang in my ears seemed to go on forever and then, perhaps because the Turks had stopped firing at us, it died down. But as it did so, the shouts of the officers and the cries of the wounded men grew louder and louder. It seemed to go on forever.

"Ah! My head! My shoulders! They're killing me!"
"My arm. It's bleeding. It won't stop!"
"You there. Get that man bandaged up!"
"Help me! I can't feel my legs!"
"You two, get a stretcher over to that man!"
"My eyes! Where am I? I can't see!"

I wrapped a handkerchief around my hand and climbed down to the lower deck where emergency lighting had been switched on in order to help the injured men. Half a dozen men lay on stretchers as doctors and medics tried to clean up their wounds and give them something to relieve their pain. The soldier nearest to me was lying on his back; a bloody red gash ran from the top of his head to just above his right eye. There was a strong smell of burnt hair and flesh about him and he rolled his head from side to side vainly trying to find some relief. A gurgling noise came from his throat and a thin trickle of blood ran down from the side of his mouth. Suddenly, he shuddered and the gurgling stopped. His head stopped moving.

"Hey! Benny's dead!" someone next to me shouted out. "Doctor, quick! Benny's dead!" An army doctor pushed his way over to where Benny Goldman lay, and laid his head close to the still body, while trying his pulse. The doctor got up and sadly shook his head. He pulled a sheet over Private First Class Benjamin Michael Goldman's face. There was no need to say anything more.

I climbed back up to the top deck to breathe some fresh air. The Turks had stopped shelling us and the sounds from below seemed muffled.

I think it was there and then that I grew up, or at least was no longer a carefree youth. The war, fighting and armies were no longer a game, an exciting adventure, a big international team game. Fighting and dying for your country were suddenly no longer just patriotic words and phrases. Men were being killed and bloodied for these ideas. Somehow it was unexpected, but it was all too real. Blood flowed and grown men screamed in agony like frightened babies. It was no longer just a case of them against us, of fighting for a free Eretz Israel. Parades, shiny uniforms and stirring speeches now seemed like a waste of time. Now, war, battle and fighting were real, as were the blood, pain and agony that I saw and felt all around me.

Suddenly I felt angry about the waste caused by war. Benny Goldman, a skinny lad from Tel Aviv, a soldier whom I'd grown to like and appreciate while doing our training, had told me some off-color jokes about camels when we'd visited the Sphinx. Days before that, he had shown me how to fold my blankets army-style in readiness for our daily tent inspections. But now he was no more.

All I knew was that he was nineteen years old and loved to tinker with anything mechanical, including his rifle. He had told me that he had two younger brothers and a grandmother in Tel Aviv and that his father ran a flower shop near the beach there. He had undergone all the training I had done, and now all of it had come to nothing. Once he had told me that after the war he planned to open a repair shop with his younger brother, but now all his talk and planning meant nothing at all. Just hopeful words and unfulfilled dreams. Nineteen years of life, of eating, drinking, breathing and planning had ended up in the agonizing pain of a terrible head wound on the deck of a British transport ship. There was neither heroism nor glory here. He had not died to save a comrade. He had died because of pure misfortune. Fate had placed him in the wrong place at the wrong time.

No doubt the army would write and inform his family that their son had died a soldierly and dutiful death, but we who saw him roll around in pain and torment knew that this was not the real truth. Bad luck had killed him. Simply put, a heavy lump of jagged red hot shrapnel had landed on him rather than falling on someone else, or even harmlessly hissing into the sea.

Later that night I met up with Nathan and Jacob. Nathan's arm was in a triangular bandage, and for once, he did not crack stupid jokes about the army and the Turks or the 750 mules that we were to use for transporting water and stores once we got ashore.

"David," Nathan told me later, looking somewhat shaken, "I've just heard that a few of our men were killed and a few others were badly hurt. They've been transferred to the hospital ship over there." He pointed out in the direction of a large ship sitting in the middle of the harbor, huge red crosses painted on its white hull and lit up, so it would not be thought of as an enemy target and be shelled. Smaller boats were transporting wounded soldiers on stretchers, which were then carefully hoisted aboard.

"I was with Benny when he died," someone next to me said. "It *was* Goldman, wasn't it? Not Goldstein?"

"Goldman," Jacob replied quietly. "He was at school with me, a year above me."

"So this is war," I sighed. "No more games and exercises."

Nathan agreed. "That's right, David. No more games and exercises."

Jacob said nothing. He was thinking of Benny, of his past friendship, and how they had sat together after school in Tel Aviv, working out homework problems in algebra.

We had arrived at Gallipoli, the place where we were to learn what it was like to be a real combat soldier.

CHAPTER FIVE
Gallipoli

For some reason unknown to us, the Turks had stopped shelling our ship as we gently pulled in alongside the landing stage. Maybe they did not want to give their positions away as the dawn light was beginning to break over the peninsula. However, the sunrise did not stop the Turkish soldiers in the hills and cliffs overlooking the harbor from firing their rifles at us, and as soon as we were ashore we had to run for cover.

"Why can't we stop them?" I asked Jacob as we took shelter behind a large rock on the beach.

"I think we've tried, but it hasn't worked. Someone has just told me that the Turks were dug in so well that it's impossible to reach them because of the steep cliffs and the *nullahs*."

"*Nullahs?*"

"Ravines. Something like we call small *wadis* back home. They have sharpshooters up there, or men with machine guns. I think we're going to have to silence them soon if we don't want to stay on this beach all the time."

And so for the next couple of weeks we stayed below and learned to keep our heads down, especially when we had to cross open and unprotected areas. There was never any silence on that beach. I was always aware of the sounds of the heavy artillery as well as the lighter and sharper shots and cracks of the rifles as the sharpshooters on each side tried to pick off the enemy. Occasionally we succeeded, and a great cheer would rise up as we saw a Turkish soldier roll over and drop down over the cliff face.

But what bothered us almost as much as the constant threat of death were the flies. They were big, black and everywhere. On the one hand you wanted to cover any exposed part of your body to prevent yourself from being bitten, but on the other hand, it was too hot and sticky to unroll your sleeves or even wear your shirt all the time.

"Don't you worry about it, mate," a Cockney soldier said to me one day as I was trying to swat some flies. "You'll soon learn to forget them. Just concentrate on keepin' your head down and you'll be all right. Them flies is nothin' in comparison to catchin' a bullet from Johnny Turk up there. You mark my words."

And during those days we did indeed learn to mark his words and ignore the flies. We were soon brushing them away without thinking about them, and soon I was working as a soldier of the Zion Mule Corps without my shirt on, like all the others.

We also, more or less, learned to ignore the various sounds of the guns – both ours and theirs – which were firing all the time. We soon learned to tell the difference between the different types: the "whoosh" made by the high-explosive shells while flying through the air before landing, or the sharp crack of the snipers' rifle shots.

One day Nathan told me that we all looked like rabbits as we dived and ducked when the shots sounded too close for comfort.

"It's hilarious," he said. "One minute you're sitting there, playing cards or peeling potatoes, and the next minute you're all diving into your dugouts. And then when it's over, you all stick your heads up to see what happened."

"And where were you when all this was going on?" I asked, feeling a bit insulted at having been compared to a frightened rabbit.

"Me? I was already in my dugout," he had the grace to admit.

We also dived for cover when the Turks sent their airplanes flying over us. Actually, the pilots were Germans who were helping the Turks, but that didn't make any difference. The airplanes were Aviatiks. These light biplanes would hover over us like hawks, spying on us in our camps and checking where we'd placed our big guns. Normally they would just fly over slowly but sometimes they would also drop a few bombs. This, of course, would make everyone stop what he was doing and dive for cover.

We had a couple of near-misses from these bombs as did the nearby Royal Naval Hospital. But of course you could never tell if you were to be next in line. "If your name's on it, that's it. There's nothing you can do about it," was what most of us believed when it came to being on the receiving end of a bomb or a bullet.

We spent most of our first days on Gallipoli unpacking the huge crates that had been sent over on the transport ships and warships, and then repacking the contents into smaller boxes. We would then strap these onto the backs and sides of our faithful mules which were our corps' special responsibility. We had 750 mules and they did not seem to care about the continuous noise of the guns and the confusion that surrounded them. I had learned to be careful not to stand behind them as I'd seen one of these animals give a vicious kick to an unlucky soldier. Someone had accidentally pushed the sharp corner of a box of ammunition into the mule's flank and it had kicked out as a reaction.

At first the British soldiers had laughed when they saw our shoulder flashes with ZMC written on them, but this banter quickly disappeared once they learned to appreciate the importance of our work.

Soon after arriving at Gallipoli it was obvious that we would have to start defending ourselves in the same way that our enemy did, by digging parallel lines of trenches to face theirs. Our trenches were from three to six feet deep, and soon we had three sets of trenches. The first ones formed our frontline, the second ones were for reserve, and a third set were supposed to be used for resting. But as they, too, were quite often fairly near to the Turks, you can imagine how much rest we had.

As the time passed, the trench system grew to be quite complicated. At first they were numbered, but later we began to give them names. The English soldiers often named them after places in London, such as Hyde Park or Leicester Square, but we of the ZMC gave them the names of roads in Eretz Israel such as Herzl Street or Jerusalem Boulevard. There were always scaling ladders for climbing out of the deeper trenches, while shorter communications trenches were dug so we could move among them without having to expose ourselves and run the risk of being shot in the head by an enemy sniper. To make the trenches even deeper and to provide us with better protection, two-foot-long sandbag walls were built along the front. Sometimes spaces were left between the bags so that we had loopholes for firing our rifles through. In front of these defenses we had rolls and rolls of barbed wire, some of which was fixed to stakes. As it was hard work preparing the barbed-wire defenses, it was usually done at night when there were fewer chances of being shot by a sniper.

In addition, lines of communication ran up and down the trench floors, and of course, the trenches had to be wide enough so that the mules would be protected as well. I don't know how good the Turkish trenches were, but after a while, ours were wide enough not only to contain ourselves and our mules, but also to provide room for our supplies, ammunition, food and water. The good thing about the trenches was that they protected us, but the bad part was digging them out of the hard rock and being stuck in them during the hot days when the heat of the sun beat down on you from all angles.

One of the things that the trench system forced on to our mole-like way of living was to see if we could succeed in damaging the enemy's trenches. Sometimes we tried by shelling them from above, or by firing specially designed trench mortars at them. These were bombs which weighed over a hundred pounds and were packed with high explosive material. We would fire them high into the air at a certain angle above the Turkish trenches. The shell would appear to hover like a hawk looking for prey and then crash down onto the enemy's lines. If we got the angle right, the death and destruction were terrible to see and hear, as rocks were shattered and the burning hot shrapnel killed and wounded the Turkish troops.

At other times we would attack the enemy from below. We would try to get as close as we could to their trenches by digging tunnels and then filling them up with explosives. When we were successful, you would suddenly hear the sound of a huge explosion echoing around the hills. This would be followed by the sounds of tons of rocks being blasted upward as dozens of enemy soldiers started screaming in agony, hit by falling rocks or shot by our machine guns opening fire on their now exposed positions.

Sometimes we were taken off our normal duties and instructed to take over nightly guard or sentry duties, or to escort other troops on various missions. I heard that Captain Trumpeldor was very pleased when this happened. When he called us together soon after for an *Erev Shabbat* meeting and *kumsitz* (sing-along), he said that Jabotinsky would also have been very proud to see us acting as regular soldiers, as he called us, and not just as uniformed handlers of pack animals.

"You may not be exactly on the front lines," he said after we had sung some *zemirot* (Shabbat songs) and had recited the Friday night *Kiddush*, "but you are first-class troops and Colonel Patterson and I are greatly honored to be your commanding officers. *Kol hakavod*, well done."

On June 4, 1915, the British army decided to "teach the Turks a lesson" and attack them on their own territory, at one of their strategic high points, about eight hundred feet above sea level, called Achi Baba. "Archy's Bubba," Nathan called it, but, unfortunately, this sinister and threatening-looking hill at the southern end of the peninsula did not prove to be like anyone's soft grandmother.

On the evening before the "big push," the British commanding officer met with his senior officers in his dugout and told them how they were to place their men. At the end of the meeting the commander added that they would be supported by the Zion Mule Corps, who would be responsible for getting water and ammunition up to the jump-off points. "But after that," he continued, "your men will be responsible for carrying their own supplies. They will also see that the same mules used for the ascent will ferry the wounded back down here to the base camp for first aid." He then answered a few questions and the officers returned to their own units to brief their men.

I woke up very early the following morning and joined the thousands of British soldiers and a couple hundred of our own ZMC men who were preparing to start the steep climb up the sides of Achi Baba. It was tough going, not only for us, but also for the stumbling mules, which we led as we carefully made our way up the rocky and spiky gorse-covered sides and ravines of the cliffs.

I must admit I was feeling somewhat nervous as we set off. This was the first time I was to take part in a battle and even though I was not a frontline combat soldier I had seen the wounds high-explosive shells could inflict on the human body. Of course I didn't tell anyone about my feelings, not even Nathan or Jacob, who were carrying their supplies a hundred yards behind me. Instead I decided to wipe my sweaty hands on my trousers and concentrate on climbing up the steep tracks as carefully as possible. I comforted myself thinking that all the ZMC men, and possibly many of the Brits with me, were feeling the same even though they did their best not to show it.

I was sure that the Turks would hear us and start shooting at us as we dislodged rocks and boulders and sent them tumbling noisily below, but nothing happened. In fact, for the first couple of hours, as we climbed up in the cool dawn, I could hear nothing apart from the panting of the men and the animals, or the sounds of our own boots and hoofs on the rocks. This was interrupted by the muttered curses of the men as they cut their hands on the sharp rocks and the spiky gorse bushes that seemed to be growing everywhere. Taking a short break to catch my breath I looked up and saw the calm waters of the Aegean Sea shimmering not too far away. The whole scene looked so peaceful as the rising sun reflected on the sea, and the grey dawn waters turned to a dark blue. I wished Yehudit could have been with me to share this but I knew that that was impossible. I promised myself that if I survived, I would tell her every detail of our time at Gallipoli (well, apart from the blood and things like that).

Soon after, we, the soldiers of the ZMC, were ordered to remain where we were and to be ready to bring up more water and ammo, or to ferry the wounded back to our base camp. After some encouraging thumps on the back and wishes of "Good luck, mate," the combat units moved off and continued their climb, while the rest of us sat in the shade of some of the larger overhanging rocks and stunted trees.

I had a strange and guilty feeling at this point. There I was, a soldier like all these others, and yet now I was sitting here in the shade away from the danger zone wishing my fellow soldiers "good luck" as they continued clambering their way up the rocky trails. I knew that many of them were very likely to be killed or badly wounded during the next three hours and I felt very disturbed as I sat down to await further instructions.

I must have dozed off in the heat, for suddenly I felt Jacob jabbing my shoulder. "David, David. Wake up! Get ready to go back down to camp. We've got to take some wounded men back to the base."

As I was pulling myself together, a large shell landed nearby, raining shrapnel and chunks of rock all over us. Without thinking, I dived under an overhanging rock, crossed my arms over my head and waited for more explosions, but none came, and soon we were busy organizing and preparing the wounded men for the rocky descent to the base camp at the beachhead below. Those who could walk, either on their own or with the help of others, did so. We lifted the more seriously wounded up onto the mules and then carefully began to pick our way down the steep slope we had climbed earlier that morning.

By now the sun was high in the sky and everything was hot to the touch: the rock faces where we put our hands for support, the metal parts of our rifles, and of course, our own bodies. We were running short of water as we'd given most of it to the combat troops. This meant that we had only a little to spare to wipe the blood off the seriously wounded men on the mules. This made both the wounded men and the animals look really grim, especially as the dried blood matted with the mules' fur. We managed to bandage some of them in one way or another, but still the blood seeped through, leaving bright red splashes of color on the white gauze.

"Bloody failure," a British soldier complained to anyone who would listen. "Led us straight into a trap."

"That's right," his mate replied. "The Turks was sittin' there waitin' for us. We was like ducks at a shooting range at the fair."

"Yeah, you're right, there. Three of me best mates was killed. Shot dead, just like that." And he snapped his fingers to show how quickly his mates had died.

"And where's the top brass when it's needed?" another soldier chipped in cynically. "Lying in bed on their boats way out there in the ocean," and he pointed to the Aegean Sea where a large flotilla of grey destroyers and frigates could be seen lying at anchor, safely out of range of the Turkish artillery.

"That's right, Jimmy. We're stuck up on these rocks, while 'is Lordship, General 'amilton is leadin' the life of ol' Reilly out there. 'E should've come ashore before all this to see what was goin' to 'appen to 'is precious troops."

He was right. The chief commanding officers lived on their ships out at sea, and all their plans were on paper. They had little idea of what all the ordinary troops, "the PBI (Poor Bloody Infantry)," were going through. Later, we heard that it was the same for the other forces who were fighting at Gallipoli. But if our commanding officers did not know what was going on, we did. We knew we had to get the wounded men back to base as quickly as possible, if they were to survive.

After climbing downhill and leading the walking wounded for two hours, we, the ZMC, together with our mules, reached the army hospital below. The men who were not too seriously wounded were treated immediately, while the others were left lying on their bloody stretchers until the doctors and their orderlies were able to deal with them. We tried to cover up their faces and wounds so that the flies wouldn't pester them too much, but soon we saw that sometimes we were wasting our time.

"Look," said Nathan, pointing to a nearby stretcher. "I helped carry him down for the past hour, and now I see he's dead."

I straightened the sheet over the dead man's face. "And you know what? At least two of our ZMC men were killed as well."

"Huh, and Trumpeldor said we wouldn't be frontline troops," Nathan said bitterly. "Now look. There'll be a couple of families, if not more, back home who'll be saying *Kaddish*."

"And I thought the British were good – that they knew how to plan an attack," I said. "Just look at this." I swept an arm around the area of the hospital tents, where wounded men were lying out in the sun, some silent, some groaning, some bloodier than others, all suffering.

"I know, David. One day if we ever have our own army, we'll have to learn from all of this."

But the high-ups, the top brass in the British army, did not. A week after this failure in which nearly one quarter of the 14,000 troops were killed or wounded, another frontal attack took place, and this one failed as bloodily as the first one. There were almost 6,500 casualties.

But the British would not give up. Pulling himself away from his beloved poetry books, Sir Ian Hamilton, the commander in chief, told the local commander, Sir Aylmer Hunter-Weston, that he must succeed this time. "We cannot have the

Turks sitting up there on Achi Baba killing off all our men just like that. I want you to take our forces, together with the Anzacs and –"

"What! That load of rude and undisciplined men?" Hunter-Weston interrupted.

"Definitely. I agree with you that those Australians and New Zealanders certainly lack discipline, but they really know how to fight. And by the way, see about taking some extra artillery with you for good measure. Altogether you will have thirty thousand men at your command."

But none of this helped. "Ol' Hunter-Bunter," as his men called him behind his back, did not take enough ammunition and the Turks, well entrenched in the village of Krithia on the Achi Baba hilltop, had no intention of surrendering. After a mix-up between the various British and Anzac units had led to failure on the first day, Hunter-Weston ordered the British warships in the harbor to shell the Turkish positions. The only difference this made was to force the Turks to retreat half a mile while the British suffered a further four thousand casualties.

Once again, we in the ZMC had to help carry water and ammunition up to the front lines and bring back the wounded men. It could not have been easy for the poor men as riding muleback over rocky ravines must have jolted them horribly, but we knew that they would have no chance of survival unless we got them down the cliffs to the first-aid stations below.

That night I wrote a letter home, or rather three, to be exact. One to my family in Tel Aviv, a copy to my father in Alexandria and another copy to Yehudit.

Cape Helles, Gallipoli
June 29, 1915

Dear Family (and Yehudit),

I have just gotten back from an "action" and I'm happy to see that most of my closest friends are still alive, although some have been wounded by bullets or shrapnel. Some others who didn't take part are resting as they are suffering from dysentery or infected insect bites.

Obviously, because of censorship, I cannot say much except to write that the flies and mosquitoes here are as much of an enemy as the Turks. They get into everything and nothing seems to help. As there's hardly any wood here we can't light fires to keep them off at night, and anyway, if we did, the Turkish snipers would take potshots at us at night as well as during the day!

In the meanwhile, I've learned how to make stick-bombs. These are made of all sorts of junk and nails and bits of glass which we pack into any can or jam jar that we find around here. We then add a fuse and throw them into the Turkish trenches. Sometimes they work and sometimes they don't. At least it keeps me busy and you can say that at last I'm learning a new trade!

Sometimes we go swimming in the bay and as I stepped into the water last time I saw a ring of black scum floating off me, so you can guess how clean I was. But since everyone else here is as clean as me, I don't feel too bad about this. In fact, some of the men are quite proud about how big and black their "ring" is!

Please don't worry about me. Despite everything I'm feeling pretty healthy and sunburned. I've lost a bit of weight and my arms are scratched from the thornbush here. Apart from missing you and the family, I really miss fresh fruit and ice-cold water.

Mother, how are you and Michael managing? Have you heard anything from Father? I haven't and I'm quite worried. All we hear here are rumors about life in Egypt and home. I hope you'll be able to write to me soon and send me some good news.

I'll write again (and another separate one to Yehudit) when I get the chance.

All the best.

Love,

David

CHAPTER SIX
January 1916: Evacuation

Two nights later I was sitting in our dugout talking with Nathan and a few friends about what we were going through.

"I just don't get it," Jonathan was saying. "I was brought up to believe that the Brits knew how to plan and fight. You know, the British Empire and all that. And just look at us here. Stuck on this wretched beach, while Johnny Turk up there, who isn't supposed to know how to fight, is taking potshots at us whenever he wants."

"I know," I said. "I've heard that we suffered over ten thousand casualties in the last two attacks alone."

"Right, and so far we've hardly gained any ground from it either."

But none of this stopped the top brass from trying to attack Achi Baba again. Like the previous attacks it failed and the Turks remained firmly entrenched on the top of their hill.

One day soon after this, Nathan came over to where we were watering the mules and attending to their wounds. "Look at this," he called out, waving a newspaper. "Just see what Hamilton has written about us."

"What? Our great white chief?"

"Of course. Who do you think I was talking about? Corporal Hamilton?" And Nathan read out a few sentences that our commanding officer had written for the American Yiddish newspaper *Der Tag*.

"*It may interest you to know that I have here, fighting under my orders, a purely Jewish unit. As far as I know, this is the first* time in the Christian era that such a thing has happened. The men who compose it were cruelly driven out of Jerusalem –"

"He means Palestine."

"I know, but Jerusalem sounds better, more biblical."

"Shhhh. Listen...*of Jerusalem*," he continued, "*by the Turks and arrived in Egypt...absolutely destitute and starving. A complete transport Corps was there raised from them, for voluntary service with me against the Turks, whom they naturally detested.*"

"Very true."

"Listen. There's more. *These troops were officially described as the 'Zion Mule Corps,' and the officers and rank and file have shown great courage in taking water, supplies and ammunition up to the fighting line under heavy fire. One of the private soldiers has been specially recommended by me* (Hamilton) *for gallantry and has duly received from the King the Distinguished Conduct Medal.*"

"And you know what I heard," Sammy Goldstein added. "Hamilton was about to accept another transport unit instead of us, but he turned it down. He said he wanted the ZMC and no other unit."

I felt very proud when I heard this and even prouder when I heard that several others and I were to return to Alexandria to help Trumpeldor and Patterson recruit some more men for the ZMC. I was also pleased that I had been chosen because I hoped that somehow I would be able to see my father and also find a way to go home and see my family and Yehudit.

"We'll be away for a couple of weeks," Trumpeldor told us. "And when we return, we'll be a larger unit altogether."

Trumpeldor was wrong. The two weeks stretched out into two months and the enthusiasm about joining the ZMC that we expected to greet us in Egypt failed to materialize. I was very disappointed. I had expected our good name to attract loads of new recruits, but what I did not know was that during our absence, the young men who had wanted to join up had been persuaded that being part of the Mule Corps would not help drive the Turks out of Palestine.

So instead of returning to Gallipoli in September with hundreds of new recruits, we brought back with us only one hundred new men. And what a "homecoming," if it could be called that, we had.

"David, you can't imagine what it's been like while you were away, no doubt enjoying yourself in the nightclubs of Alexandria," Jacob said, as I pushed my way into his cramped dugout.

"What? You didn't try for Achi Baba a fourth time?" I asked.

"No, thank goodness. The Brits seem to have given up on that one."

"*Tov*, good. So what's been happening then?"

"Well, quite a lot of our ZMC men have been killed or wounded."

"By snipers?"

"Yes, and also by shells and high explosives. And then a couple drowned in the bay and a few others were badly injured when they fell down *nullah*s and things like that while they were out on night patrols."

"Sounds like you've really had it rough," I said quietly.

"Rough! David, that's an understatement. Like we've been having a party here. And on top of what I've just told you, we've all been suffering from sunstroke, mosquitoes, flies, dehydration and everything else you can think of. This place has become a real hellhole."

"That's not new."

"I know. But it looks like the Turks have really become better fighters, that is, better than what the top brass thought when we first came here. They've got a really good Turkish commander, a general or colonel, called Mustapha Kemal, and a German General von Sanders who is helping him train his men," Jacob said.

"That's right," Nathan added. "So watch it from now on, David. You have to keep your head down during daylight. Even more so than before you left. If not, the Turks will put a bullet right through it."

"Yes, and they've even shot some of our mules."

"What on earth for?"

"Because I suppose they think that if there are mules around, then there's water and ammo for the men. So shoot the mules and you're shooting the enemy."

"Well, it does make sense, I suppose. I mean from their point of view."

"True. But, you know, the mules saved some of our lives a little while ago."

"What do you mean?"

"Well, we were out on patrol one night, looking for where the Turkish lines might be a bit weaker or less well defended, when a shell went off nearby. Some of the frightened mules managed to escape from their traces and started charging ahead. Suddenly all hell broke loose. The Turks, who were nearer than we thought, ran out of their trenches, and our mules charged into them! If they hadn't done that, I think we'd have all been killed. We had no idea we were within such easy range of the Turks."

Despite Nathan's story of the mules, I was very sad that night. Sad for what had happened to my friends and the ZMC. I had known over a dozen of the men who had been killed and wounded while I was away, including Reuven Weitzmann. He had lived near us in Tel Aviv and had been a good friend of Yehudit's younger sister, Sarah. I was also sad to see that we were doing very little to hurt the Turks. At this rate it would be years before we would be able to force them to leave Eretz Israel.

Next morning I heard some more bad news. Patterson, our commanding officer, would be leaving Gallipoli because of illness and Trumpeldor would be replacing him as the commander of the ZMC. It's not that I didn't like or trust him, it's just that I felt that as long as Patterson was with us, we had a stronger and more personal connection with the British top brass. Nathan and Jacob agreed with me.

"What we need," Jacob said, "is a commander like the Jewish one the Aussies have."

"The Anzacs?"

"Yes, they've got this chap, Monash. Brigadier General John Monash. He's Australian and before he joined the army he was a civil engineer. It seems that he's much better at organizing things than the Brits and that's why their top brass don't like him very much."

"That's right. And also because he's a civvy in the army and not a career officer."

"And probably because he's Jewish as well."

"Well," Jacob said, "I don't care. I just wish he was down here at Cape Helles with us and not up there at Anzac Cove."

"And is it going any better up there?" I asked.

"Is it hell! They're also suffering like us, but at least this Monash fellow is trying to help them. Not like Hamilton and Hunter-Bunter who spend all their time keeping out of range on their precious warship out in the bay."

I could see that all my friends who had started off so keenly at the beginning of the year were now feeling really fed up and bitter. Everything had gone wrong: thousands of men had been killed or wounded and nothing had been gained. We were getting shot at all the time and still the Turks, whom the British had despised as lousy fighters, were commanding the heights above us. How much longer would we be able to put up with this situation?

As the days passed, it started to become cooler. The hot, dry days turned into a short fall which was followed by a cold and wet winter. Where the ground and trenches had been hot and dry, now they were cold and muddy, as the rain flowed off the hilltops onto our sandbagged defenses. The rainwater turned into rivulets and torrents and these flooded our damp and gloomy trenches and dugouts. Before, the lack of success had made us miserable; now the weather increased our wretchedness. Living on and clinging to the exposed side of a soaking cliff, where you could be shot at any moment, was no fun.

"Well, at least there are no flies now," I said one day after I had returned from patrol duties. "But I wonder when the brass hats will realize that we're wasting our time here in Gallipoli."

"Why? Would you prefer to be on the Western Front?" Nathan asked.

"That's right," Jacob added, "stuck in muddy trenches facing the German artillery."

I grudgingly admitted that Gallipoli was perhaps a somewhat better alternative, but our stay on the peninsula seemed to be getting us nowhere. In the meanwhile we made a few improvements to our dugout and succeeded in constructing a fireplace and chimney stack out of old cans. We burned bits of driftwood and charcoal which we found near the back of the field bakery. We also hung up some heavy khaki-colored material to act as a curtain-door and this kept most of our precious heat inside.

Luckily, our commanding officer had also decided to try to improve our conditions by allowing us to go and find enough suitable square-shaped rocks to build some sort of house that we would be able to use when we were off duty. Some of us were sent off to find suitable building material in an abandoned Turkish village and while we were there we came across a great surprise.

"Nathan! Jacob! Come and see what I've found!" And there, half-buried among the fallen rocks and timbers of a smashed-up house, was a beautiful slab of marble with a *Magen David* carved in the middle!

"What do you think it is? Where do you think it's from?" Jacob asked.

None of us had any idea but we brought it back with us to our base camp and used it as part of the front wall of our new rest house. I don't really think I'm superstitious, but when shells and bullets were flying around, none of them ever hit our building or wounded anyone nearby.

Although we didn't know it at the time, Hamilton and his commanding officers had also seen that the Turks were far from surrendering and that the British were getting nowhere fast. This fact was also pointed out during a visit from their superior officers from the War Office in London. These included the commander in chief, Field Marshal Lord Kitchener, a man whose face with its beady eyes and mustache appeared on thousands of British recruiting posters. At a high-level meeting two major decisions were made. After having lost thousands of men in a failed attack in the north, the ineffectual General Hamilton would be replaced by General Sir Charles Monro. It was also decided to cut our losses and bring the Gallipoli campaign to an end.

Soon after this strategic decision had been made, we of the ZMC, together with other units in our area were told that within the near future the evacuation of Gallipoli would begin. However, this was to be no ordinary evacuation, but one that was designed to fool the Turks into thinking we were still in our trenches. It was also to be carried out as stealthily as possible with the aim of saving as many lives as possible.

"At last they're thinking about us," Nathan said cynically, "the PBI, Poor Bloody Infantry."

"Shhhh, be quiet! I want to hear what's been planned."

We were informed that perhaps some soldiers would be killed during this evacuation, but that it would still be worth it. We were to destroy as much of our stores and equipment as possible without attracting the Turks' attention and were also told to light as many cooking fires as in the past, even though several thousand men were to be withdrawn very soon. In other words, we were to give no hint of what we were planning to do.

"What do you mean by that, sir?" a soldier from the 29th Division asked.

"Your instructors will give you all the details." And at that point an instructor stepped forward holding a rifle. He laid it flat over some sandbags.

"Now look here carefully," he ordered. "I will place two empty tins, just like the ones you've been making bombs out of, next to this rifle. Note that one tin is higher than the other. The top one is full of water and is now set to drip slowly into the bottom one. See?"

We craned our heads forward to see what he was trying to show us. The instructor continued. "Now when the bottom one is full, its weight will pull this piece of wire here," and he pointed to a small length of wire that had been tied around the rifle's trigger, "and fire the rifle. Now watch me demonstrate."

He poured some water into the lower can, which pulled down the wire. The rifle went off and we all clapped. It was a bit like watching a magic show.

"*Nu*, at last they've planned something that works," Nathan said.

"Let's hope so," I said. "I've had enough of this place."

Soon after we were given the orders that we would be leaving that night. We went to pay a visit to the graves of our fallen comrades and said *Kaddish*. Sadly, and with feelings of guilt, we then cut the throats of our faithful mules, so they would not fall into enemy hands.

For once, the British plans succeeded. And it was even more successful than they had foreseen. During the night of January 8, 1916, eight months after we had first arrived, we quietly sneaked out of our sodden dugouts, set our rifles to fire as we had been shown, left explosive booby traps all over the place and, under the cover of a moonless and cloudy night, made our way silently down to the beach. We boarded the transport ships that were to take us away from Gallipoli, forever. Not one soldier was killed that night. It was only months later that we learned that over 46,000 Allied troops had died there in vain, and that thousands more had been badly wounded in this futile campaign.

When the news of our evacuation got back to Australia, a poem called "Anzac" was published by a poet calling himself "Argent."[1] Two verses of it went like this:

> *And all our trouble wasted!*
> *all of it gone for nix!*
> *Still…we kept our end up —*
> *and some of the story sticks.*

---

1. Argent, "Anzac," in Oliver Hogue, *Trooper Bluegum at the Dardanelles* (London, 1916).

Fifty years on in Sydney
they'll talk of our first big fight,
And even in little old, blind old England,
possibly someone might.

Besides the other casualties, several of our ZMC fighters had been killed, over twenty were badly wounded and four of us (but not me!) were awarded military honors, one man even receiving the DCM, the Distinguished Conduct Medal.

The next day we of the ZMC were assembled together and informed that we were to sail back to Alexandria. There it would be decided what would happen to us. We also learned that we could not return home to Palestine as the Turks were still in control of the country. That night it was with mixed feelings that I joined in with the others to celebrate our newfound freedom away from the trenches. On the one hand there were no more deaths, flying bullets and mosquitoes, but on the other hand I wondered what we had really accomplished. Not having anything special to do, we began to feel bored and hung around waiting for news. And of course everyone wanted to go home. For my part, I wanted to see my family – and Yehudit especially. I hadn't heard from them in ages. As always in army life, there were fresh rumors every day.

"We're going to fight the Turks in Palestine."

"No, we're being sent to France."

"To the Western Front?"

"Yes, near Paris, or somewhere like that."

"That's not true. I've just heard we're going to be sent to England to help train Jewish soldiers there."

But the truth was completely different. General Hamilton was removed from his command over his failure to beat the Turks at Gallipoli, and General Maxwell decided that the ZMC would be sent to Ireland. There we would be used to put down the anti-British riots that the fighters for Irish independence had started.

It did not take us long to tell Captain Trumpeldor that we had no intention of doing the British government's dirty work in Ireland. We had joined the army to fight the Turks and free Palestine from their rule. Our Jewish commander smiled and promised that he would pass on our message to General Maxwell. He said he'd also speak to Jabotinsky who, for the past few weeks, had been trying to interest the War Office and the Foreign Office in London in organizing a new combat unit composed of Jewish soldiers. We, of the ZMC, would be the core of this new unit.

After this meeting with Trumpeldor, nothing happened for a while. We hung around Alexandria and tried to keep ourselves busy. At first it was a relief to be able to walk around upright and exposed and not feel that you were a sitting duck for a sniper's bullet, but after a while boredom set in. After all, how many weapons retraining and drilling exercises can you do? I also tried to find out where my father was, but the British army's red tape defeated me and all I learned was that he had not yet returned home.

Then, one day toward the end of May 1916, Captain Trumpeldor ordered us to assemble in the main square of the camp. He informed us that since we had refused to be used to help put down the civil war in Ireland, the British government saw no point in keeping the ZMC as a separate unit. "As a result," Trumpeldor finished, his voice full of emotion and his thick Russian accent becoming even stronger, "the Zion Mule Corps is no longer needed within the framework of the British army and so it is to be completely disbanded."

This was followed by cries of disbelief. There were other cries of "I told you so." But before things could get out of hand, our commanding officer raised his hand for silence.

"That was the first thing I had to tell you. The other is that since January this year, compulsory conscription has come into operation in Great Britain. This means that any soldier here who was born in Britain or who has British parents must join the army. Those men here in this category will be sent to Britain for further training. Thank you. But..." and here he held up his hand again as a wave of noise and discussion began to overtake the assembled men. "But, before we are to be disbanded, I wish to say, that as the commanding officer of this very special unit, the Zion Mule Corps, I have been very proud to have led you. I have also been very proud of your past efforts, both for ourselves and also for the sake of the Jewish people and the Zionist dream. So let me finish with our traditional blessing, *chazak ve'ematz*, be strong and of good courage."

And so there I was, nearly twenty years old, a Jewish war veteran in a now disbanded unit of the British army. There was nothing for me to do in Egypt and I could not go back home to Tel Aviv because the Turks were still there. Besides, I was still subject to British army regulations. I did not want to go back to New York, and so I agreed to be sent to Britain, a country I had never been to, to be retrained, but for what?

Would we, the men of the ZMC, be kept together or not? Would we be returned to Palestine to have another crack at the Turks, or would we be sent to fight the Germans on the Western Front? Only time would tell.

CHAPTER SEVEN
July 1917: The Jewish Legion

It was a typical summer's day in London, cool and overcast, with a promise of rain, when Lieutenant Colonel Patterson knocked on the door of the adjutant general's room in the War Office. The door opened, and a uniformed secretary took Patterson's hat and greatcoat and pulled up a chair for him.

Patterson began. "I received your telegram, sir, and came as quickly as I could get away."

"Ah, yes. You've been commanding the Royal Dublin Fusiliers," Sir Neville Macready noted.

"That's right."

"But now you are here," Sir Neville continued. "Let's get down to business, shall we? By the way, were you informed why I asked you to come and see me here at the War Office?"

"No, sir. All I know is that I heard it's something to do with my past experience at Gallipoli and the Middle East."

"You heard correctly. The reason I've asked you here is to tell you that the government has decided at last and, if I may add, after a lot of badgering from Mr. Jabotinsky, whom I believe you know, to form a Jewish Legion."

"Something on the lines of the Zion Mule Corps, sir, that took part in the Gallipoli campaign?"

"Yes and no. Yes, because the soldiers will be Jewish. And no, because it will be a combat unit and not a service unit like your ZMC was."

"And where do I fit in with this, sir?" Patterson asked. He was interested. It sounded much more challenging than sitting at his desk in Dublin, filling in forms and attending endless meetings.

"You, sir, with your past experience and knowledge of the area will be the commander of this newly formed Jewish Legion. That is, if you agree."

"I certainly do, sir. And how large will this unit be? Battalion? Brigade?"

"Well, Patterson, it will be fairly small at the beginning, but the aim is to turn it into a brigade in the end."

"So I would become a brigadier," Patterson said, trying to conceal his pride.

"And," continued Macready, "this Jewish Legion would have its own logistics, badge, special food..."

"Kosher food, sir?" Patterson asked.

"Yes. Kosher food would be supplied, and all the Jewish holidays and festivals, like their Jewish New Year and Day of Atonement, would be observed."

"I see. And where would we be serving, sir?" Patterson did not relish another minor mutiny on his hands as had happened when his soldiers had refused to put down the civil disturbances in Ireland. "Only Palestine, sir? Not Ireland?"

"Only Palestine, Patterson. On that you have my word. I've already contacted General Allenby, who will be the overall commander in the Middle East. Does that meet with your approval, sir?"

"Yes, sir. It certainly does. But I do have a couple of requests to make."

"Fire away."

"The first is, can this Jabotinsky chap join us? And if so, can he be given the rank of lieutenant, that is, not as an honorary rank? I believe he may have lost it when the ZMC was disbanded."

"And the second request?"

"That Captain Trumpeldor, the officer who served under me at Gallipoli, also serve in this new Jewish Legion. He did a very good job out there."

"Well, Patterson, I'm not sure about that one. You see, I've already checked it out with the War Office and it seems that they are not very happy about having an officer with only one arm holding such a responsible office."

"I see. But he did such excellent work when he filled in for me at Gallipoli, sir, you know, when I was ill and had to be rushed home. And of course," he added as an afterthought, "Lord Nelson didn't do such a bad job commanding the British navy a hundred years ago, did he? Together with only one arm and one eye."

"All right, Patterson. I understand. I'll see what I can do, but I can't promise anything will come out of this. And by the way, Patterson, what role do you have for this newly commissioned Jabotinsky? From looking at pictures of the man, he doesn't look much of a fighter to me. Looks more like a schoolmaster, if you see what I mean."

"I'd like him to be responsible for recruiting fresh troops, sir. As you may know, he speaks English, Russian, Yiddish and even Hebrew, sir."

"Hmmm. Sounds ideal. Maybe he'll be able to persuade all those Russian Jewish refugees in England to join the army. God knows, we need some more men after all those disasters on the Western Front."

"Yes, sir. But I wouldn't say that aloud, sir. No one's going to volunteer to join an army that's lost thousands of men in France, sir."

"That's true enough, Patterson, though you needn't put so fine a point on it. At any rate, now that conscription is obligatory, the Russian Jews will have to enlist."

"Yes, sir. Or the Home Office will send them back to Russia."

"And they certainly won't want that, will they?" Sir Neville said, smiling. "But in the meanwhile, you'll have those ex-ZMC men of yours to start with and we'll see about recruiting some more men. Yes, that idea you mentioned about using this Jabotinsky fellow sounds a good one. I'll certainly follow it up."

And so I, David Levi, together with Nathan and Jacob, three of the hundred ex–Zion Mule Corps soldiers in England, became some of the first to be recruited into the newly formed Jewish Legion. Supplied with our army rail passes, we took the train to Plymouth, from where we made our way to Crown Hill Barracks for refresher courses and training. It was nothing like the "good old days" in the Gabbari camp in Egypt where we had started our military careers. Our officers were much stricter with us, and the discipline as well as the punishments for breaking the rules were much harsher. In Egypt, we would have been given extra kitchen duty or guard duties for breaking rules or for having dust in our rifle barrels, but here in Plymouth we ran the risk of being sent to the local military prison instead. In Egypt, under the hot sun, we had taken breaks for drinks and cigarettes, but here in Plymouth this was unheard of.

"Levi! You're late for parade. Report to my office at 1100 hours!"

"Yes, sir."

"And remember, 1100 hours is 1100 hours, and not half a minute after!"

"Yes, sir."

We spent our days going through all the regular courses for infantrymen. Woken up at the crack of dawn, we would eat an early breakfast, "with no bacon and eggs for you lot," and then assemble on the parade ground. There we were divided up into smaller groups and sent to revise and improve our musketry skills. We were also instructed how to look after our new Lee-Enfield rifles and how to march and drill. We also learned how to signal and use our bayonets.

Fixing the bayonet on the rifle was a bit tricky. Our instructor, a big bull of a man, would bellow at us, "When I shout 'Bayonets,' you whip 'em out and fix 'em!" He would time us on how fast we fixed our bayonets as well as how fast we could take our rifles apart and then put them together again. Then we had to repeat this exercise, blindfolded. He taught us the following verse which we sang to the tune of "D'ye Ken John Peel."

> *Now, dress by the right, boys, and get into line,*
> *First by numbers, and then judging the time,*
> *For you whips 'em out, and whops 'em on,*
> *And lets 'em bide awhile,*
> *That's the way you fix yer bayonets in the morning.*

And God help any soldier who let any dirt get into or onto his rifle! I saw grown men (including me) grow weak at the knees at the sight of a speck of dirt in the barrel or in the sliding bolt mechanism! And if our rifles had to look bright and shiny, so too did our belt buckles, fittings and boots. We soon learned that the army phrase "spit and polish" was no empty saying. We even bought, with our own money, our own special polish and cleaning materials called "Soldier's Friend" and "Blanco."

At first, the physical training was a bit tough, especially as I hadn't really stretched my muscles for some time. But after the first few weeks, I was as fit as I had been at Gabbari before setting out for Gallipoli. In the end, Nathan and I would see how many push-ups we could do within five minutes. Although he usually beat me, I was always the first past the tape in running races and in the interbattalion athletic competitions.

Strangely enough, I quite enjoyed drilling, although I thought that most of it was a complete waste of time. My time at Gallipoli had taught me that once a soldier is on the battlefield, he has no time for parade-ground maneuvers. Such exercises had nothing to do with the cliff faces of Gallipoli, or the muddy stretches and trenches of the Western Front. I knew we would be sent to the Middle East and I also knew that "Left, right! Left, right!" would not be too useful there, either.

However, if I thought drilling was really a waste of time, the course on saluting seemed even more so. We had to attend lectures on how and whom to salute. The different ranks of officers had to be saluted in different ways, and if we were carrying a rifle at the time, then we had to salute in a different way. A sentry carrying his rifle at the slope had to place his right arm across his body and hold the rifle butt with his left hand. Then if all of this were not enough, we also had to learn how to give special salutes to field-ranking officers, and even to groups of soldiers. The final salute we had to learn was the very special one that we were to use if ever we had to salute the king, King George V! I could not really imagine that one taking place.

"Just imagine," our instructor said, "one day you might have to go to Buckingham Palace to receive the V.C., the Victoria Cross, from the king himself." We were not impressed.

But at least the course on signaling was more interesting. We learned different sorts of codes, such as the Morse code, and how the Indian Morse code differs from the one used in England. We also learned how to send different semaphore signals, using colored flags, although I doubted whether we'd ever really have to use this information.

"Just imagine," Nathan said one day after we had finished learning how to send numbers by semaphore. "There I'll be, standing in the middle of a battlefield, bullets and shells flying around, waving my arms around with these flags and suddenly an enemy sharpshooter puts a full stop in me. Very useful!"

Our instructor also told us about whistle and bugle signals, but at least he was honest enough to add that these were not very important or practical as the sounds of machine guns and high-explosive shells would drown out any whistles or calls we made. We agreed with him, and then proceeded with the last part of the signaling course, the international code for flag signals.

"Now this really is a waste of time," I whispered to Jacob. "These flags are for sailors and not for us who are going to get stuck out somewhere in the desert." But it was fun to learn, and it made a break from sentry and kitchen duties, as well as the never-ending job of keeping our rifles clean.

The most exciting part of our training was practicing with our bayonets. We were told that they were of the sword-bayonet type, just over seventeen inches long and weighing one pound, two ounces. We had to run toward our targets, which looked like stuffed sacks, and yell bloodthirsty noises as we cut and thrust our bayonets into them. Our instructor would stand at the side and yell at us, "Kill 'im! Jab 'im in the guts! Come on, man, get stuck into 'im! I want to see blood!" And then after a session of this, we'd have to go back and clean up our rifles – again!

One thing that I noticed in our new barracks was that we tended to split up into very different groups. Most of my time was spent with Nathan, Jacob and the others who had been with me in the ZMC, while the others tended to stay with their friends who had received permission to transfer from other regiments. I noticed that most groups seemed to center around those who spoke the same language, and I suppose this was natural. We had "Galitzianers" and "Litvaks" who spoke their own type of Yiddish, and they would poke fun at their rival group's language, who would then mock them in return. There were many tailors in the English group from Whitechapel and the East End of London and one day to my amazement I heard two of them having a noisy argument about the various makes of cotton and needles! Of course, when we wanted to say something that we did not want our British officers to understand, then naturally Nathan, Jacob and I would say it in Hebrew, with some Yiddish phrases thrown in.

One thing that surprised our instructors, though, was that we Jewish soldiers did not drink – that is, we did not drink alcohol.

"Don't you lot drink?" Sergeant Smith, our firearms instructor, asked when he saw some of us sitting near, but not in, the building where the camp's bar had been.

"Yes, sir," I answered innocently, looking up from the letter I was writing to Yehudit. "Tea, coffee and milk."

"No, I mean booze. Y'know, beer, whisky an' stuff like that."

"Well, we drink wine with our Sabbath meals," I said. "And sometimes we drink some wine after *shul* on Shabbat, er, Saturday."

"*Shul*? What's that?"

"Synagogue."

"Oh, like the Catholics."

"No, not really. But that's about all the alcohol we drink."

"Ah, so that explains why they closed the bar down," he said, and walked off to find a bar that was open outside the camp.

Despite the lack of liquor, however, we found plenty of ways to keep ourselves entertained, and we even developed quite a cultural life. Many of our number were expert musicians and they formed a musical ensemble and performed concerts for us. Word spread in the Plymouth area and the men were requested to play for local events! We also had lots of interesting lectures. Lieutenant Jabotinsky was a rather literary fellow, and he spoke often on various subjects, such as the poet Bialik. We even received a visit from the famous Rabbi Abraham Isaac Kook of Jerusalem, who spoke about the duty of a Jewish soldier.

In the meanwhile, we heard how two British offensives in Palestine had failed. It seemed that both Generals Dobell and Murray had sent their men into frontal attacks against the Turks who had faced them from well-defended trenches.

"Just like the Western Front, David," Nathan sighed. "They send our men over the top against lines of heavily defended positions, you know, with lots of machine guns, and the result is that thousands of them get killed."

"I know. I heard that we lost over six thousand men there, three times more than we did against the Turks."

"And did you hear that the British ran out of water for their horses? They couldn't use them for charging the trenches."

"Yes, I heard about that. And then some Turkish forces sneaked around the back and caught the Brits off guard."

"But didn't the Brits use their tanks out there?" Jacob asked.

"Yes. They tried but they kept overheating and getting all jammed up with sand," Nathan replied.

"Just like our rifles," I laughed.

"True, but this was much more serious." Then Nathan added, "General Dobell has been sacked, if that's any consolation."

"So who is the new commander?" I asked.

"General Allenby. I've never heard of him, but I hope he'll be better than Dobell. Otherwise we'll never get the Turks out of Palestine," Jacob said.

Fortunately, Allenby was better than Dobell. This general, who had been a cavalry corps commander and nicknamed "The Bull," had led the Third Army on the Western Front. He had partly defeated the Germans at Arras and Vimy Ridge, and had now decided to use new tactics to smash the Turkish lines of defense which stretched from Gaza to Beersheva. Instead of attacking head-on, as Generals Dobell and Murray had done, he had used more men than before and this had forced the Turks to stretch out and weaken their own lines. He had also made sure that he'd had enough water for his men and their horses, even building a railway line to make sure that his men were well supplied with ammunition, food and water.

General Murray had tried – and failed – twice to take Gaza. Allenby had hatched a plan to take Beersheva first, with the help of a special trick: he planted false documents for the Turks showing British plans to launch another assault on Gaza! The ruse was carried out even to the point of sending a small force to shell Gaza, distracting the Turkish army from the real invasion point at Beersheva.

The battle for Beersheva took place on October 31, 1917. This included a successful charge by the Australian cavalry which smashed through the Turkish lines and overran the enemy trenches, machine-gun emplacements and wells. The Turks began to retreat to the northeast, and we all felt very relieved when we heard this.

"Nathan, don't you realize that this is one of the first victories over the Turks? We might even get them out yet."

"I know, especially as the Brits have also captured Jaffa."

I thought for a moment, and imagined English soldiers walking around Jaffa and Tel Aviv, like we had done in Alexandria and Cairo, and suddenly I felt very homesick. I thought about my parents and wondered whether my father had ever made it home. I thought about Yehudit and wondered whether she still cared about me after all this time. If I ever got home again, would we still be friends? Would we have a future together, or had we grown too far apart during my absence? I was still feeling low when Nathan and Jacob burst into our hut two days later and found me dozing on my bunk.

"David! David! Have you heard the latest? The British government has suggested that the army organize several Jewish regiments which will include foreign Jews now living in England."

"That's not new."

"I know, but now we're not going to be on our own like we were in the ZMC. We're going to be part of the Royal Fusiliers, the 38th Battalion. Even Jabotinsky agrees with this. They're hoping that enough Jews will volunteer so that they'll be able to form another battalion as well."

"Yes," Jacob added. "And that means that we'll have a regular recruiting office in London and we'll also have our own regimental badge. It will look something like this." And Jacob drew a sketch of a badge he'd seen on an army document. It looked like a round ball with flames coming out of the top. There was some writing on it.

Badge of the 38th Battalion Royal Fusiliers

"Looks like a bomb that's about to go off," I commented.

"Well, say what you like, but maybe we'll succeed in bombing the Turks out of Eretz Israel, especially with the support of Patterson and the Brits. And I think Jabotinsky is going to be one of our commanders."

From then on, our numbers started growing and about forty new recruits joined us every week. A few weeks later, Nathan and Jacob burst into our hut again.

"David! Listen to this. The Brits have published this letter saying they are for the idea of having a Jewish state in Palestine! Our own state in Eretz Israel! Isn't that great?"

"What do you mean, a letter?" I asked, now fully awake.

"Here, listen. It's in the paper." And Jacob began to read to read it out:

"November 2, 1917.

"Dear Lord Rothschild –"

"Why Lord Rothschild?" I interrupted.

"I don't know. Maybe 'cause he's rich, or he's the only famous Jew they know. Anyway, be quiet and listen."

"Dear Lord Rothschild,

"I have much pleasure in conveying to you, on behalf of His Majesty's Government, the following declaration of sympathy with the Jewish Zionist aspirations, etc. etc."

"Go on."

"Ah, yes. Here we go," and Jacob cleared his throat and continued.

"His Majesty's Government view with favor the establishment in Palestine of a national home for the Jewish people, and will use their best endeavors to facilitate the achievement of this object, and so on, and so on."

"That's fantastic! So now we really do have the British on our side, not just a few pro-Palestinian officers and men like

Patterson," I said. "That should really scare off the Turks. By the way, who signed this letter?"

"Lord Balfour, the foreign secretary."

"Not Lloyd George? I know he's pro-Zionist."

"You're right. Anyway, I don't suppose Balfour would have written this letter if the prime minister hadn't agreed with him."

So now we had the support of the British government. We hoped that this support would turn out to be something real and not be just an empty government declaration, a piece of paper.

Our luck, or at least that of the British army, seemed to hold as it began forcing the Turks back up north. On December 11, we heard that Allenby had broken through to Jerusalem and had even entered the Old City through the Jaffa Gate. We read that, as a sign of respect to the holiness of the Old City, he had gotten off his horse and walked through the gate on foot. This simple but dramatic act had left a deep impression on many people. Later, Allenby told reporters that he had not felt that it would have been suitable for him to enter the Holy City as a conquering general on a horse. He had also given orders that Allied flags were not to be flown over the main buildings and, in order to avoid offending the Muslim population of the Old City, he had sent some Muslim troops from India in the British army to guard their holy places. He also had read out a proclamation of goodwill in English, French and Russian, as well as in Greek, Hebrew and Arabic. The Roman Catholics were especially excited about this victory and rang their church bells in London and in Rome.

"David, do you know what I heard?" Jacob said, a little later. "I heard that the Arabs actually think that Allenby will be good for them as well."

"How come?"

"Because they say that when you write his name in Arabic it comes out something like *Allah-an-nabi*."

"So what?"

"*Allah-an-nabi* is Arabic for something like *the Prophet*."

As we read the newspapers and the magazines we were filled with jealousy. "We, not the Brits, should be there, chasing the Turks out," I said.

"True, and they need us, too. I mean, it seems like maybe the Brits aren't as strong as they used to be," I mused. "After all, we were forced to sneak away from Gallipoli in the middle of the night and the Turks won the first two battles in Gaza."

"That's right," someone else added. "And look what's happening now on the Western Front. Thousands have been killed at Ypres, Loos and on the Somme. Thousands. And for what? Just for a few hundred yards of muddy territory and smashed-up pill boxes."

He was right. During that grim winter, thousands of British troops were killed at Ypres and Passchendaele on the Western Front. It seemed that only in the Middle East were the British making any progress as they fought their way north from Jerusalem, in the direction of Damascus. And all this time, Nathan, Jacob and I, and hundreds of others were burning to join in. Was it fair, I thought, that I should be stuck in a British army training camp in the south of England when I should really be fighting for my homeland in Eretz Israel?

CHAPTER EIGHT
From London back to Alexandria

I was still feeling somewhat useless and down in the dumps a few days later when Jacob's friend, Danny Cohen, ran to tell me something while I was standing on the central parade ground.

"David, don't forget to be here at three o'clock," he said.

"Why? What's happening then?"

"There's going to be a special parade this afternoon. Patterson or somebody else has something important to tell us."

"How do you know?"

"Well, first of all I heard about it when I was in the office about half an hour ago, and secondly, haven't you noticed all those big fancy staff cars coming and going all morning?"

I had to admit that I had not. I had been stuck too deep in my own thoughts and feelings of frustration to notice who was coming and going. And besides, since when does a humble soldier like myself pay much attention to what the top brass are doing? Experience had taught me that, unless their decisions had anything to do with me directly, it was a waste of time to concern myself with generals, colonels and the like.

Anyway, at three o'clock I was back on the parade ground, standing at ease with what I hoped was a perfectly spotless rifle, waiting to see what would happen. After the usual "Attention! At ease! Attention!" we were ordered to stand at ease until Lieutenant Colonel Patterson arrived. After five minutes of waiting and standing in line as a light wind blew around us, a large staff car rolled onto the parade ground and our commander stepped out. After more "Attention! At ease! Attention!" and exchanges of salutes, we were ordered to stand at ease.

Then, without wasting any time, Patterson informed us that our long months of training were over and that various high-ranking officers thought that we were ready for battle. As our training was complete, he continued, we would soon be leaving our barracks at Crown Hill and would be sailing for Egypt in order to fight the Turks on what they considered their own territory.

Suddenly all the troops standing on that parade ground in Plymouth, from privates like me to sergeants and officers, let out a great cheer. This was greeted by Patterson and the commanding officers standing next to him with large smiles, and they made no effort to restore the usual order of the parade ground. We calmed down after a few minutes, and Patterson, holding up his hand for complete silence, then told us we would be going by train to Southampton in a few days, and from there we would be sailing to France.

"But," he added, standing stiffly to attention, his baton under his arm, "half of you will be going to London by train tomorrow for a big parade which is to be held there. The names of the men involved will be posted on the notice board outside my office at 1800 hours tonight. That is all. Parade dismissed!"

That night I learned that Nathan, Jacob and I were to go to London, but Danny would be left behind. He did not seem to mind at all. "At least I won't have to polish my boots every ten minutes," he said. "Or check my rifle for dirt."

"Or for London fog!" another soldier called out.

But I was pleased. It would mean a break from our usual routine, and it also meant that I would get a chance to see the capital city of Britain. I hoped that we would have a bit of free time before or after the parade to go sightseeing.

But before any of this happened, Sergeant Abrahams announced that every NCO and soldier like myself would first have to have an army haircut. This was known as a shearing parade, as all our heads were clipped very closely. "Like lambs to the slaughter," one cynic muttered. "But at least I won't have to pack a comb with me."

The next day we arrived at Paddington station and, after the usual pushing and shoving, formed into lines and set out for the business area, the City of London and Whitechapel. It became clear why the army authorities had arranged for us to march through the mainly Jewish area of Whitechapel. Large crowds stood on the sidewalks cheering, and it seemed as I looked up that all the windows above the shops (which had names in English and Hebrew lettering) were full of people cheering us in English and Yiddish. It certainly made me feel very proud to be a Jewish soldier in a Jewish battalion. It made me stick out my chest even more and march even better than I had at Crown Hill. It was also good to see people throwing flowers at us as we marched down Commercial Road in the direction of the historic Tower of London.

"I wish my family and Yehudit could see me now," I whispered to Jacob.

"Yes. And my parents as well," he agreed, and we both stuck out our chests even further.

That night we slept in the tower, "a great honor for you lot," and later we were told that quite a lot of lads from the East End had been so impressed by our parade that they had volunteered to join our battalion.

The next day was even more impressive. We marched to the Mansion House, the Lord Mayor of London's residence, this time with fixed bayonets glinting in the sun. We also had a band to lead us and hundreds, if not thousands, of Londoners cheered us as we proudly carried our regimental colors as well as the Union Jack and a large flag bearing the Star of David. We came to a halt in front of Mansion House and Lieutenant Colonel Patterson made a short speech. An important rabbi also made a speech, and blessed us and prayed that we would win our ancient homeland of Eretz Israel back for the Jews. He finished his speech saying, "*Hashem oz l'amo yiten, Hashem yivarech et amo bashalom*, the Lord will give strength unto His people, the Lord will bless His people with peace." He then presented a Torah scroll to the battalion.

Following this presentation, Lieutenant Jabotinsky gave a speech and said, "Now we will obtain the Land of Israel in a manner befitting us as a nation, only if blood is shed for its liberation, and only if Jews bear arms." There were a few more speeches, after which we re-formed our lines and marched to Waterloo station for the train to Southampton. There we met up with those who had stayed behind and we all got ready to cross the English Channel, our first stage on the way to the Middle East.

I remember that we left England for France during the first week of February 1918, sailing on HMS *Antrim*. It took us just over a week to arrive at Taranto in the south of Italy by train, and we enlivened our journey by drinking some cheap French wine and by practicing our schoolboy French on some unfortunate passengers. The naval port at Taranto was very impressive and I would have loved to shown its beautiful harbor and castle to Yehudit. I must admit I was feeling quite happy, because just before leaving England I had received a letter from her. It wasn't very long, but it showed that she was still thinking of me. She didn't write anything specific about my mother and brother, wrote that they were well "under the circumstances" and admitted she hadn't heard any news about my father. Although this made me sad, what did make me happy was that for the first time she had signed her letter "Love, Yehudit."

While we were there, hanging around and waiting for the ship to take us to Egypt, we had to attend another ceremony, although this one was more religious than the one in London.

"I suppose it's because we're getting nearer the Holy Land," Nathan whispered to me out of the side of his mouth, as we stood stiffly to attention.

As before, Lieutenant Colonel Patterson and Lieutenant Jabotinsky were there on a raised platform, together with Rabbi Falk, who presented us with a special ark for the safekeeping of our Torah scroll. He closed his speech with the words, "As long as you have the ark with you, the good Lord will protect you."

Patterson nodded his head in agreement and added that the presence of the ark on our ship would also protect us from the German submarines that were lurking about in the waters of the Mediterranean Sea.

While the authorities were organizing the last-minute preparations, we had a few days to enjoy the Italian sun in Taranto, and wander around like tourists, between parades and drills. And all this time we had to keep our rifles spotless for the sudden but expected inspections!

We left Taranto early in the morning on February 25 and as we set sail for Alexandria on the SS *Leasoe Castle*, I found myself looking forward to being back in Egypt – well, at least the Middle East – again.

"Nathan," I said, as we sat in our cabin. "Going back to Egypt makes me feel as if I'm going home – or at least most of the way. But I wonder what we'll find when we eventually do get back to Tel Aviv."

"If we do," he replied somewhat cynically.

"Of course we will. It's just a question of when, and what happens on the way," I said, trying to sound more confident than I really felt. "Let's hope for the best. Come, let's go up on deck and see who's the first to see Alexandria. That's where the fun's going to start."

Later that evening we heard that the Zionist leaders David Ben-Gurion and Yitzhak Ben-Zvi had joined the American branch of the Jewish Legion together with hundreds of others. They were due to sail to England before meeting with us in the Middle East, as the 39th Battalion. Two battalions of Jewish fighters in the British army out to rid Eretz Israel of its Turkish occupiers! And after four hundred years, too. That was certainly a good thought to go to bed with that night.

Seal of the American Jewish Legion

CHAPTER NINE
Eretz Israel Again!

We arrived in Alexandria at the end of February and were very happy to be on dry land again. Let us just say that the sea and my stomach were never the best of friends.

"But at least it's sunny now, and not too hot," I said to Jacob.

"Yes. It's better than that grey Plymouth and London weather. Let's just hope it stays like this."

But of course it didn't. As the weeks passed and we learned to fight in desert conditions, the pleasant warm spring weather turned into the hot, dry desert climate that everyone expects of Egypt. We sweated in our army uniforms as we marched, drilled and carried our packs and rifles, as well as learning how to use our various weapons, practicing ambushes and other military skills. Of course these included improving our accuracy and shooting speed at the rifle ranges, as well as learning how to throw hand grenades efficiently.

It was also about this time that we first met the Americans of the 39th Battalion. Naturally there was much friendly rivalry between the two battalions. Many of us who had fought with the ZMC mocked the newcomers as greenhorns, while they on their part thought that we were exaggerating when they heard us brag about our heroic (as we described them) exploits at Gallipoli. In fact, they were right, but naturally we would never admit it! However, as the time passed, we learned to get along well and respect each other, and the rivalry was never really serious.

They told us about their time in London. "The Brits there sure knew how to make us Yanks feel good," one of their sergeants said to me. "We were taken around the city and then we had a parade right through the center of London. Boy, that was really good. Everyone was looking at us in our British army uniforms with our *Magen David* badges."

"And then we started singing some American and Russian army songs as well," his friend added. "And the crowds really went wild. They started throwing flowers and candy at us and some girls even ran out to kiss me!"

"That's right," one of their sergeants said, smiling happily at the memory of it all. "And later we went to a big ceremony at Covent Garden. Y'know, all speeches and food. Even Lord Rothschild was there."

"Yeah. And then we went to see the Houses of Parliament. Heck, that is sure some building. Nothing like it back in Kansas."

"Well, there's nothing like Kansas here, either," I said. "Except that maybe the desert is as flat and it goes on for miles."

"Yes, and if we're talking about the desert, don't forget to keep your water bottles filled up," Jacob said.

"And keep your hats on," I added, feeling a bit superior. "Otherwise the sun here will cook your brains."

And so we carried on with our training, had competitions in marksmanship and played interbattalion games of football with our new American and Canadian rivals.

From time to time we went to the large and impressive synagogue on David Street where the chief rabbi of Egypt delivered sermons before blessing us and our endeavors in freeing the Holy Land from the Turks. The best part of the synagogue services though, was that afterwards we would be invited back to the homes of people in the congregation for a Shabbat meal. Naturally, any food after army food was a vast improvement!

Later we went by train to Cairo, and from the station we marched a few miles to our new training camp at Helmieh. While we were there, General Allenby, the commander in chief of all the British troops in the Egyptian Expeditionary Force (EEF), together with the Duke of Connaught, reviewed us on parade.

A few weeks later we were given a break for Passover, and Lieutenant Colonel Patterson, who knew his Bible, finished his speech and dismissed us with the words: "You are here now in Egypt like the Children of Israel were in the past. But next year, *L'shana haba'a b'Yerushalayim!* Next year in Jerusalem!"

"Or Tel Aviv," Nathan whispered to me.

"And Yehudit," I added.

It was funny to hear our commanding officer speak in Hebrew, especially with a slight Irish accent, but all the men were pleased and broke into applause when he stepped down off the platform.

As we were eating breakfast about one month after Passover, an officer entered the tent and told us to be on parade in half an hour. There we were informed that our period of desert training was over and that night we would be boarding a train for the Palestinian front.

Palestine! Eretz Israel! Home! Yehudit!

"At last, we're going home," I said to Nathan and Jacob.

"Yes, but before that we've got another parade. So make sure your water canteen is full and your rifle's clean! You don't want any more kitchen duty, do you?"

"No need to remind me," I said, thinking of the mountains of potatoes I'd peeled, to say nothing of all the big cooking dixies I'd had to scour. And all because of a few specks of dirt stuck in my rifle barrel!

The parade that Nathan had mentioned was not held in our camp, but out in the desert. First we were put on the train – in this case, an open-roofed freight train – and then we set out in an easterly direction for our homeland. At about one o'clock in the morning, we stopped right there in the middle of the desert and were ordered to "stand to" in our usual parade-ground formation.

We stood at attention as Lieutenant Colonel Patterson, wearing his dress uniform and all of his medals, made a speech about it being our historic duty to liberate the Holy Land from the Turks, now that we had crossed the border from Egypt into Palestine.

"We're home!" I whispered jubilantly to Jacob.

"Right, but I wish it was warmer," he said, shivering a little in the chilly desert breeze.

Someone then played a solemn melody on a trumpet and Rabbi Falk led us in prayer. Now I knew I was back after three years, and his words had special meaning for me. We then got back onto the train where we huddled together in the open carriages in order to keep warm.

I must have fallen into some kind of sleep because the next thing I remembered was someone nudging me in the ribs and shouting, "David! Wake up! Look, there's Lod! Look at the houses and the fields. They seem bigger than when I saw them last."

"But don't they look neglected? The Turks seem to have smashed everything up."

"Look! Look! The Judean mountains!" And Jacob pointed to some mist-covered heights in the distance.

The train pulled into the dilapidated station at Lod and, after collecting all our kit, we marched the half dozen miles to Sarafend, the barracks where we were to be stationed before being sent to the front. I think I held myself even more proudly than when I'd marched through Whitechapel as I thought that here I was, marching in a Jewish battalion, here to fight for the freedom of Eretz Israel. And all the time I was looking closely at the faces of the people by the side of the road to see if I could spot anyone I knew. It was certainly a strange feeling to know that I was back home and within a few miles of my old house in Tel Aviv, and yet I could not return home and see my family and Yehudit. It wasn't fair. So near, and yet so far!

As the Bible teaches us, we rested on the Sabbath, our first in Eretz Israel in three years, and attended morning service and *Kiddush* which included prayers written especially for the occasion by the chief rabbi of Egypt.

A few days later, following an inspection parade by General Allenby, we marched east toward Samaria. That night, soon after we had started digging our defense trenches we suddenly came under shellfire from the Turkish artillery.

"Quick! Get down!" I yelled at the two men digging a trench next to me. They seemed to have frozen on hearing the loud bangs and simply stood there like statues, completely immobile. However, my shouting must have gotten through to them for they ducked down immediately, covering their heads with their arms.

As I threw myself to the ground, memories of the Turkish shelling at Gallipoli flooded my mind. The explosive noise of this attack now overwhelmed us. For many of the men who had not been in the ZMC at Gallipoli, this was a new experience and some of them panicked. Half an hour later, when it was all over, Nathan and I found one of our men – a tailor from

London – cowering behind a rock repeating the *Shema* prayer to himself over and over again. Nothing in our training, either at Crown Hill or Alexandria, had prepared him for the real thing. It took us some time to calm him down and, in the end, we gave him a spade and a place to dig a slit trench, thinking that while he was digging, it would keep his mind off the shelling. "Start digging here, and make it really deep."

"Yes, so you can duck down into it," I said, hoping that digging in the rocky ground would keep him really busy.

That night, Jacob and I and two others were sent out on patrol to check that all our sentries were in position. Our lines along the hilltops of Samaria, or *Shomron*, as we preferred to call it in Hebrew, stretched for miles from Abu Ein to Jaljulia. The Turkish lines were about two miles to the east, and although we could not see the enemy, we could easily spot the muzzle flashes when they fired their artillery in our direction.

"At least the no-man's land between us is dry," an older soldier who had joined us in London commented.

"What do you mean by that?" I asked.

"Well, out there on the Western Front, in France, near the Somme where I was for a good few months, no-man's land was all muddy and craters. The chances were that if you took shelter in a shell hole, you'd probably drown in it."

"That's right," his friend added. "That is, if the rats didn't eat you first."

And then the pair of them began to tell Jacob and me about their Western Front experiences.

"This place is a piece of cake," the skinny one said. "It's nice and dry and hot during the day, and there aren't any rats."

"Yes, and your mates here are Jewish," his friend added with a smile.

"True, but you didn't have mosquitoes back there in France," I said.

"You're right, but I still prefer them to the mud and the German shells of the Western Front."

A few days later, after taking up our positions in our sector of the line, we were ordered to occupy Abu Ein as a forward observation post. As this deserted Arab village was in the middle of no-man's land, we had to move in under the cover of darkness. All our actions such as building defense walls, digging trenches and keeping an eye open for the Turks, while recording their movements at the same time, had to be done as silently as possible.

Each week a different company of men would be sent in, and it was not easy. In addition to carrying out their duties, they also had to be constantly aware of the ever-present threat of sniper fire. So everything had to be done while crouching down and making sure your head was protected by some sort of wall or bank of earth and rocks. At least one soldier died the week after I left; he had exposed his head above a wall for a few seconds too long.

The other problem was the mosquitoes. We really suffered from them at Abu Ein, as they came from the smashed-up old sewer pipe that ran through the village. The mosquitoes certainly preferred the valley to our hilltop positions and, when the week spent in Abu Ein was over, the men would return to our lines covered with bloody bites, and more than one man came down with malaria, or some other sort of infection.

One evening, as a group of us who were not on patrol or sentry duty were sitting around behind a wall playing cards and chatting, a sergeant came over to us.

"Listen, you lot. I've just heard that we'll be pulling out of here soon."

"Why? When are we going?"

"Yes, and where?"

"I don't know exactly. But I know we're going to be moved to the east, maybe to Jerusalem or to the River Jordan."

The sergeant had gotten it right. A few days later, on August 9, we of the 38th Battalion were transported to Ramallah, a small Arab town just north of Jerusalem. We stayed there for a couple of days but did not enjoy the break.

"It's just like Cairo or Alexandria," Nathan complained. "Dirty, stinky and full of flies."

I agreed. "And the whole place is full of pickpockets."

"And if they're not doing that," Jacob added, "they're busy trying to sell you cheap junk or torn postcards."

So, as you can guess, we were very pleased when we received orders that early on August 12 we were to leave Ramallah and march to Jerusalem. Jerusalem! The Holy City! I had not been there for at least four years; the last time had been a few months before the Turks had deported us, when my father had taken me with him on a business trip. We had wandered around the crowded and shady streets of the Old City *shuk*, buying a few cheap souvenirs from the various market stalls. After that we had walked through the religious area of Meah She'arim and then continued to the modern Western-style suburb of Rehavia in the New City. From there we could see the walls of the Old City, which my father had told me were built by an Ottoman leader four hundred years ago with the very "modest" name of Suleiman the Magnificent!

Since General Allenby had taken over Jerusalem from the Turks, it was not dangerous for us to be there. We used the free time we had to visit the ancient Wailing Wall, the only part remaining of the Second Temple. I must admit that I was a bit disappointed there. There was not much room in front of it, just a narrow alley which was crowded with dirty beggars who wouldn't let you pray as they were so busy begging for alms. The whole area was full of garbage and quite smelly. It certainly did not look like a holy place, and I was quite glad to escape to the more open streets on the outside of the Old City walls.

While I was waiting for some of the others, I sat on a low stone wall and wrote a letter home.

Jerusalem (by the Old City)
August 13, 1918

Dear Mother (and Yehudit and anyone else),

I am writing to you from just outside the Old City. It is a strange feeling to be writing to you from here because I am so near but yet I am not allowed to take any time off to come and see you. I promise you that as soon as I am allowed to do so, I will be on the first train or army truck (or even donkey!) that goes to Tel Aviv!

We arrived here yesterday and have been very warmly received by the Jewish population here. They lined the streets and cheered us loudly, maybe even more loudly than the Jews of London when we marched there. Everyone kept pointing to our Magen David shoulder badges and to the Magen David on our flag. It really was a special feeling to be a Jewish soldier marching in a Jewish battalion, and in the Holy City as well!

By the time you get this, we will have left Jerusalem to go east, but of course I can't tell you where. The weather is very hot and dry during the day and we all drink lots of water and fruit juice.

Before we got here we took part in some fighting near Abu Ein, but I suppose you read or heard about that. Do not worry, nothing happened to me there, except that I got bitten to pieces by mosquitoes and that I cut my leg on a sharp rock. (It's OK now.) It's left me with a funny-looking scar, but nothing else.

How is Father? I haven't heard from him for ages. Is he still in Alexandria, or was he able to come home after the Turks surrendered in Tel Aviv in November? How is Na'omi and how is she doing with her studies? Is she still seeing the same boyfriend — you know, the one I always called Spotty-face?

Please don't worry about me. I am well, but I have to finish off now if this is to catch the post in time. Will write to you again when I can.

Lots of love,
Shalom,
David

p.s. *Yehudit, I'm sorry, I can't write a separate letter to you this time, but please write to me c/o the British Army PO as soon as possible. I'm dying to hear all your news.*

I went off to find the army post office and rejoined Nathan and Jacob waiting by the Jaffa Gate.

"Well, David," Jacob said. "I hope you've seen what you want to here, because I've heard we're leaving tonight."

"I know. We're going to join the rest of Allenby's men. As far as I know, we'll be somewhere near Amman, but we won't know exactly where till later."

We hurried off to our meeting place opposite the central post office on Jaffa Road. One day in Jerusalem. That's all we were allowed. According to the rumors – and army life is full of them – we would be taking part in a major battle against the Turks. But rumors are rumors. Anything could happen in the future. All we could do was wait and see. "Or march and see," as Nathan said, trying to be his usual witty self.

CHAPTER TEN
Action on the East Bank

General Allenby certainly had an advantage over the Turks when he planned to attack them in the late summer of 1918. The Turks had three armies which included 32,000 infantry, 2,000 cavalry and over 400 pieces of artillery while we had 57,000 infantry, 12,000 cavalry and 540 pieces of artillery.

Allenby's plan to rid Eretz Israel of the Turks was simpler and more daring than the one he had used in his campaign to defeat the Turks in the south. He had attacked them in Beersheva and then continued to attack them all the way north until he had reached Jerusalem. Now, on the eastern bank of the River Jordan, his aim was to surround each one of the Turkish armies separately, while gaining control over the railroad system at the same time. This was an important part of the enemy's supply network. To carry out this plan Allenby needed infantry battalions like ours and the 39th as well as other cavalry and artillery units. Our task would be to trick the Turks into sending their troops into places where they would be unnecessary, and then attack the rest of their weakened lines of defense.

We of the 38th Battalion, together with some of the 39th under Colonel Margolin, were to be placed under the command of the Anzac commander, General Chaytor, I learned later after we had returned to Jerusalem. But now I had the feeling that we were all keyed up to take our own part in the fighting, our Jewish part in freeing Eretz Israel after hundreds of years under Ottoman rule.

We marched out of Jerusalem through the Damascus Gate to the north of the Old City and set out in an easterly direction for Rabbath-Amman on the eastern side of the River Jordan. As we marched, we could feel the heat and the pressure build up, even though the sun was setting in the cloudless western sky behind us. It was as if each rock, as well as the road surface itself, was giving out its own heat to cook us as we descended into the Jordan Valley.

"Nathan," I said, wiping the dust and sweat off my face for what seemed the thousandth time, "this is the hottest weather we've ever had. And it's past midday too."

"You're right. It's even worse than Egypt."

"What wouldn't I give for some good ol' grey skies and English drizzle right now!"

"Oh, for foggy Plymouth!" Jacob cried out, swatting a mosquito off his face. "At least we didn't have these devils to deal with there." And he held up the dead body of a bloody mosquito to show that he'd won a very minor battle.

"Another enemy bites the dust," I said.

But Jacob's "victory" made very little difference as we kept marching down into the Jordan Valley. It may have been a bit greener than the rocky hillsides around Jerusalem, but the scrubby plants hid clouds of mosquitoes and flies who were only too happy to bite and annoy us. Many of us pulled up our collars as we marched – anything to give these flying pests fewer chances to attack us. We knew the Turks wanted to attack us, but we had not counted on this small, buzzing enemy that was our human enemy's ally.

Some twenty miles on, we reached Jericho, where we had a short break. The ancient town was a dirty and dusty spread of single-story buildings centered around a mosque or two, and an open area used for the weekly market. Piles of camel and donkey dung were everywhere, and of course they also attracted clouds of angry buzzing flies.

"David, do you think this is the same Jericho that Joshua destroyed in the Bible?" Nathan asked as we sat under a date palm.

"I suppose so. But I can't see any walls today. All I can see are dirty old buildings and flies."

"And camel dung," he said, watching a soldier neatly side-step a pile of it. "I just hope we don't have to set up camp near here."

"Well, the Turks did until the Brits chased them out a few months ago."

"So the Brits can have it," Jacob added, "even if Joshua did get here first."

Fortunately Jacob's wish came true, but our situation did not improve. We were ordered to start marching east again, and so set out for Wadi Mellaha. This was a really stinky and swampy area, the vegetation taking its water from the River Jordan, which meandered about in the valley. If we had thought the flies and the mosquitoes were a nuisance before, they were nothing in comparison to what we heard and saw now. Their continual buzzing and biting was beginning to drive me crazy, but suddenly all of this faded away as we became aware of the Turks, who started shelling us. The explosions shocked and deafened us, and caught me completely by surprise, especially as I had been concentrating on my mosquito misery.

"Get down!" I yelled at Nathan, who seemed to be as shocked as I was. I grabbed his leg and pulled him down.

"Jacob! Quick, crawl over to the rocks over there and keep your head down!" I did not really need to tell him what to do, but I suppose it was a reaction to seeing high-explosive shells flying around near my best friends.

We sheltered behind some rocks and, after a while, the shelling stopped. Our officers read out a roll call, and I was relieved to learn that no one had been killed or seriously injured.

"Next time we might not be so lucky," our captain said. "Now they know we're here, they might try their luck again later. So be on your guard, and keep your heads down."

That night we continued marching until we linked up with General Chaytor's Australian and New Zealand (Anzac) mounted division. Some of them had fought at Gallipoli and, in the traditional way of all soldiers, we began swapping yarns and stories about the past, remembering dead friends and deadly situations.

"Do you remember that young Aussie lad who used to take jerricans of water up to the top and then bring down wounded men on his donkey?"

"Who? Simpson?"

"Yes. I wonder what happened to him. I hope he was at least given a medal."

"I don't know about a medal, but I do know that he was shot by a sniper."

"Was he killed?"

"Yes."

"That was bad luck. I heard he was only about sixteen years old."

"Yeah. Signed up underage."

"And what happened to that Turkish general? You know, the only one we thought was any good."

"Mustapha Kemal?"

"Yes."

"Well, he's here now. I mean in Palestine. He's in charge of their seventh army."

"And where are they?"

"In the north. Near the Hills of Ephraim."

During the daytime we rested as much as possible, trying to find shade from the sun, while doing boring jobs like cleaning our rifles (for a change!) and building defense walls out of rocks. This itself was pretty dangerous, as often there were scorpions hiding under the rocks. It didn't take us long to learn to kick the rocks before picking them up and checking to see if anything nasty crawled out from underneath, before using them for our defenses.

"You might complain about the heat and the flies," an English corporal said to me as I was busy swatting flies one day. "But back there, on the Western Front, it's much worse, I can tell you."

"How so?"

"Well, to start with, it often rains there and then the ground turns into one big mud bath. And believe me, mate, gettin' mud out of your rifle is much worse than gettin' sand out. And cold? It's bloody freezin' out there at night. Goes right through you. No, mate. You count your blessings. 'Ere it's a picnic, I can tell you."

One week later his "picnic" came to an end. A Turkish sniper shot him straight through the heart just as he was getting ready to go out on a night patrol.

These night patrols were the real action. We would prepare ourselves for them by smearing dark stuff on our faces and covering up the shiny bits of our rifles with mud, which we hated to do since we knew we'd have to clean up our rifles again after our patrol. The idea of all this was for us to get as close as possible to the Turkish defenses, kill as many of the enemy as we could, and then get back to the safety of our own lines as fast as possible without being caught or detected.

One evening, Jacob and I and ten others were chosen for a night patrol. Nathan wanted to join us, but couldn't – he was lying in the medical tent with severe cramps in his stomach. Captain Grossman was to be in charge, and before we set out he called us over to his tent.

"This time," he said, "the aim of the patrol will be different from that of the last ones you were sent on. Then, the aim was to kill as many of the enemy as you could and also cause as much chaos and confusion as possible at the same time."

"And this time we're going over there to give them *Chanukah gelt*?" a cheeky soldier from the 39th asked.

The captain did not laugh. "Don't be funny, Corporal Weinman. The aim, this time, is to get as close as possible as before, but instead of killing their sentries, we want you to grab three or four of them and bring them back here. Alive."

"For interrogation, sir?"

"Yes, Private Cohen. Our intelligence boys want to know something about their plans and positions. Any questions?"

There weren't any. We all knew what to do.

"So I'll see you back here in three hours. Make sure you've got everything ready: rifles, ammo and water bottles. And don't forget to cover up anything shiny. There's going to be a full moon tonight and you don't want it shining on any of your gear, now, and giving you away, do you? And yes, make sure your water bottles are filled to the brim. We don't want them sloshing about making a horrible noise. And finally," he added, "make sure your boots are well wrapped up with rags so you won't make a noise on the rocks. And for God's sake, make sure your boots are tied up tightly. Last week one idiot's came undone and the noise his loose boot made nearly gave us away. When you've done all that, you will all report to Sergeant

Goldsmith who will be holding an inspection parade to see that you're all ready before you go."

Later we returned to the captain's tent, where another soldier and I were told to leave our rifles behind; we would be taking machine guns instead. I was not very happy about this, but I could not argue. The machine gun was much heavier and more cumbersome than my rifle. It was also more awkward to move quietly over the rocks in the dark carrying it.

"Right, from now on," Captain Grossman said after he was satisfied with our preparations, "no talking, unless it's absolutely necessary. All communication will be done by hand signals."

We set off in single file, taking great care to be as silent as possible, and I couldn't help but think back to the first time I had gone into action at Gallipoli and how scared I had been then. Now I was feeling much more confident and hoped my feelings were helping our general morale, especially for two of the "new boys" who were with us. We knew the Turks were busy doing the same thing and, more than once in the past, the silence of the night had been shattered as one of our night patrols had collided with an enemy one. Then the night air had echoed to the sounds of exploding grenades, gun butts on bodies, and the shouts and groans of the dying and the wounded. The trick of course, was to surprise the enemy before he surprised you. I just know I was feeling so alert and tense that I was sure that the Turks, wherever they were, could hear the beating of my pounding heart!

Suddenly, not far ahead of me, somewhere on a low hill to our left, I could hear a light metallic sound – something like a rifle bolt being drawn. We crouched down, bent on one knee, rifles at the ready, frozen in our positions, each one of us scanning the area. The silence was so real and heavy that you could touch it.

After what seemed like ages, the signal to move on came. It seems that one of the men behind the captain had gotten up quickly and somehow a loose bullet in one of his pouches had fallen out and bounced onto the rocks below. He was sure the Turks would hear it as it fell, its sound echoing in the valley where we were hiding. I was sure, loose bullet or not, that the Turks had heard us, and were now setting the sights on their rifles. But we were lucky. They had not heard us, so we carried on up the wadi, wide-eyed, crouching and alert. I felt like a cat in the night. A cat with a machine gun!

Then a hand signal from in front told us to stop and to remain in a crouching position. From where I was, behind a large rock, I could make out Captain Grossman's hand pointing to where a Turkish sentry was chatting to two of his friends. Silently, the captain indicated that we should spread out and surround them. We knew from our past training exercises that, at a certain moment, we were to move in, grab and gag the men and then drag them back to our positions. Naturally this had to be done as quickly and as quietly as possible. After all, we didn't want to raise the alarm and allow their comrades to move in and rescue them.

Silently we slipped off the safety catches on our weapons and waited. Crouching down, I could feel the sharp pins of cramp crawling up the calf muscles on the back of one of my legs. I was in agony. I tried to move it without making a sound, though I was dying to cry out. Just as I was about to push my leg back, I saw the rest of our men creeping toward the chatty Turkish sentry and his friends, outlined on the hill and framed by a clear moonlit sky. They continued with their conversation, completely unaware that a dozen pairs of eyes, together with a dozen rifles and machine guns, were trained on them like stalking tigers. Slowly we advanced up the hill, our eyes on our prey all the time. It was hard work keeping as low as possible, especially for me carrying my heavy machine gun. It seemed to want to bounce on the rocks all the time, but I succeeded in keeping it under control.

Suddenly, at a prearranged signal, six of our men leapt forward, two to each Turk, pulling them down to the ground, while gagging their mouths at the same time. The rest of us kept watch, ready to open fire if any other Turks appeared, alerted by the commotion. This time we were lucky. Our three Turks had chosen to gossip some distance away from their comrades, who were completely unaware of what was happening to Kemal, Mehmet and Suleiman.

After tying their hands behind their backs, we took them back to our camp, again as quietly as possible. All we needed now was to be attacked by the enemy after having kidnapped some of their men! Carrying the machine gun, I was at the rear covering our retreat. It was difficult climbing down the rocky hillside while looking behind me for much of the time, and twice I nearly fell over. But of course I had no choice. The others were counting on me, and we all made it safely back to our camp. We handed over our prisoners to some intelligence officers whose job it was to interrogate them and then went back to our own tents.

I felt a great sense of relief and pride that I had come through my first action since Gallipoli without being wounded and I felt that I had handled myself well. Later, Captain Grossman called us over to his tent for a meeting.

"You men did a good job," he said, passing a bottle of schnapps around. "One of the men you took tonight was an officer. What he was doing chatting to his men in the middle of the night, we don't know, but no doubt we will soon enough. Usually their officers and men don't mix, but I'm sure we'll learn what plans they were cooking. As for you men, you may have the rest of the night and tomorrow off. Report back to me here tomorrow evening at six o'clock. Good night."

I looked around me. We were all smiling and feeling very relaxed. It was probably a combination of relief and schnapps! Suddenly the tent flaps were pushed aside and Major Rabinowitz entered. This normally cheerful officer looked very grim and turned to Captain Grossman.

"Captain, may I interrupt you," he asked, and before waiting for an answer, turned and faced us. "I'm very sorry to have to report this to you at this time of night, especially after your successful action earlier this evening, but the other patrol we sent out tonight was not as lucky. We've just found out that two of our men, Corporal Hershkovitz and Private Solomons, were captured by the Turks. Hershkovitz was shot, and it looks as if Solomons was tortured. He probably died from the loss of blood. We found their bodies about an hour ago. The Turks had dumped them on the hill north of here, probably as some sort of grim warning of what they would do if they caught any more of our men."

Our feelings of relief and satisfaction vanished. We all knew the two men. Joseph Hershkovitz had fought with the ZMC at Gallipoli, while Mikey Solomons had come over from New York with the 39th. He used to have an endless supply of jokes which he told in Yiddish with a very heavy American accent. All his jokes started with him giving a dig in the ribs of the person standing nearest to him, and asking, "Hey! Have you heard this one?"

"I think that in light of this, we should all observe one minute's silence. The chaplain will be holding a service for them tomorrow. I'll let you know when." He saluted Captain Grossman and ducked out of the tent leaving us in silent thought. Slowly we went back to our tents thinking of our two dead comrades. From now on, any future patrols would be a much more serious affair.

Unfortunately, Hershkovitz and Solomons were not our only casualties in the sticky Jordan Valley. By the time we were given the order to move east, some seven weeks later, only 150 out of those who had started, that is, eight hundred men, were still able to fight. Many of the others, including our officers, had died of malaria, and over twenty men had been killed, wounded or captured.

CHAPTER ELEVEN
Umm Es Shert and Es Salt

Soon after this we were told about our next mission. We were to secure the ford at Umm Es Shert by the River Jordan. The basic plan was for the Anzac cavalry to cross the Jordan as part of Allenby's spearhead after we, of the Legion, had captured it.

It was *Erev Yom Kippur* and we had a brief *Kol Nidre* service. I must admit that during the prayers, I was feeling a bit morbid and wondered if this would be my last *Yom Kippur*. I had heard over the army grapevine that our next mission was going to be a tough one, much more dangerous than anything we had done so far. Like soldiers throughout history on the eve of battle, I didn't tell anyone of my fears and just hoped that if I had to die, it would be quick and painless and not a long and bloody agony.

After the service we were assembled in a large beige-colored tent to hear our final instructions. We, of the 38th, were to be commanded by Lieutenant Colonel Patterson while our rival battalion, the 39th, would be led by Colonel Margolin, a Russian-born officer who had come to live in Eretz Israel after having served in the Australian army.

As usual we were told to check our weapons and see that our ammunition pouches and water bottles were full. Above all, we were to remember that we were Jewish fighters fighting for our own Holy Land. Our next mission would be making an important contribution toward bringing freedom to our ancient homeland.

"And remember, men, all of this will depend on how you carry out your mission. If you succeed, you will bring military glory to your nation and to the British army – in particular, the Fusiliers, the King's Rifles and the 38th and the 39th Battalions. But if you fail – well, I won't say anything about that."

Later that day, as the sun, looking like a blood orange, was setting over the jagged mountains to the west, we set out in the direction of the River Jordan. Nathan, Jacob and I marched together as usual, but as soon as we left our base camp we could see that our progress toward Umm Es Shert would be slow.

Nathan started coughing. "Can you see anything, David, anything in front of us?" he asked. "The Turks are trying to slow us down. They're burning off all the grass and shrubs."

And it was true. The heat and smoke of the burning vegetation, together with the dust, made it very difficult to keep up a good pace. And the thick air stank from the overpowering sweet and sickly smell of the dead horses and camels that the Turks had left behind, their bodies covered with clouds of buzzing flies. But we had to control our feelings of nausea; the main aim was to be on our guard against the exploding shells that the Turks kept firing at us. It seemed pretty clear that capturing the ford would not be easy.

"Get down!" I yelled suddenly to Jacob and pulled him down as a shell came flying over, hissing through the baking air. It fell a couple of hundred yards behind us, sending up thick clouds of acrid-smelling smoke, shards of rock and dust. I could even taste the fine dust in my mouth. I got up, but saw that Jacob was still lying on the ground.

"What is it?"

"It's my leg. When you pulled me down I fell on a sharp rock," he said. "Look, it's bleeding." I could see that his pants were torn and a patch of blood was spreading over his uniform.

I searched in my pack and fished out a bandage. "Here, don't worry. We'll put this on and you'll be all right." After cleaning him up we rejoined our slow-moving column, Jacob limping a little.

We now covered our mouths and noses with damp handkerchiefs as the smoky, stinking air got worse, but the relief did not last long. The heat soon dried them out and in any case, we preferred to save our precious supplies of water for drinking.

As we made our way over the rocky terrain, the Turkish shelling got louder and nearer. We could hear the screams of wounded men and of their horses hit by hot, jagged pieces of flying shrapnel. Some of the enemy soldiers were sprawled over the rocks and boulders and others lay on the dusty tracks in unnatural positions. When Nathan and I stopped to help a fellow soldier from the 38th, we were yelled at to keep moving.

"But he needs water and some bandages!" I shouted back.

"Forget it! Just keep moving. One of the medics will come for him later."

However, before moving off to regain our column, Nathan and I propped the wounded man up against a smooth boulder and wished him *b'hatzlacha*, good luck. I also managed to give him a drink and left a large triangular bandage with him in the hope he'd be able to use it.

We continued like this for the next couple of hours. I felt as though I was marching in a nightmare. My legs were moving automatically, just moving one in front of the other without thinking as I stepped over or around boulders, broken pieces of military equipment or dead horses that the retreating Turks had left behind. Empty brass shell cases lay everywhere, and every so often you could hear the metallic clang among the sounds of boots on rocks as a soldier kicked one of them on his way to the front. And while all this was going on, the Turks never let up firing at us, which caused us to duck and dodge among these scenes of destruction.

Suddenly I was jerked out of my dream-like march. "Halt!" We had reached a point overlooking the River Jordan. Somehow I had made it. I shook my head and looked around. If I thought before I had already seen some grim scenes of death and destruction, they paled in comparison to what I saw and smelled now. Dead horses and smashed-up equipment bearing Turkish army markings lay everywhere: boxes of ammunition, broken wagons, wheels, rifles and bullets. Destruction was spread out over the whole area, the bullets and shells spilled out among the rocks and the desert thornbush. Now we could see dead Turkish soldiers lying where they had fallen. In their bloodied uniforms some were still holding their rifles. They looked rather like broken khaki-colored dolls. But these dolls had once been men, living creatures like us.

By now we were all completely exhausted. We had marched and clambered, climbed and slid over miles of rocky country and did not need to be told twice to halt once we could see the Jordan. "You will set up camp here for the night. Post sentries but be ready to move out at a moment's notice. Each watch will be manned by at least two men. Remember, the enemy might still be lurking around out there, so keep your eyes peeled."

Gratefully we fell to the ground, ate a few biscuits and drank some water. It was not much of a meal but we didn't care. Luckily I was not on sentry duty that night and even though I asked myself how could I sleep amid all the death and destruction, the next thing I remembered was Jacob shaking my shoulder trying to wake me up.

"What?" I muttered, somewhat annoyed. "It's still dark."

"I know, but it won't be for long. So wake up and get moving. We've been given orders to fall in. And, my friend, count yourself lucky. I've been up half the night on sentry duty."

Getting up in a half daze I gathered up my kit, splashed a little water on my face and made my way among the rocks and smashed equipment to where my unit was getting ready. We climbed down the valley to the Jordan and started marching alongside the river. From time to time we could hear the crash of artillery shells but, because I was still either half-asleep or because they seemed to be falling far away, I didn't pay too much attention to the noise. Sometimes we passed the fallen bodies of the Turkish soldiers in their ill-fitting uniforms, a few of whom had been attacked by vultures and wild animals. The stench was awful, but I found to my surprise that I was beginning to get used to anything.

"Is this what rescuing the Holy Land from the Turks is like?" I asked Nathan. He nodded and continued marching. It was a different picture from the noble one I had painted in my mind's eye back in the days of the Gabbari camp in Egypt. Then I had seen myself strutting into a captured town as a conquering hero. Sometimes this scene had me riding a proud high-stepping horse, but now here I was, marching along a dusty and rocky track, keeping an eye out for enemy snipers and high-explosive shrapnel-filled shells. My mouth was dry and my feet were baking. I was feeling pretty tired and could see that Nathan and Jacob were feeling the same. The only good thing was that there were no mosquitoes during the day; but the annoying flies made up for them. Again, I marched as in a dream and only seemed to wake up when we received the orders to "Stand down." This I did with great relief, moving into the shade of a large, round, sand-colored boulder.

We rested there for some time, filling our water canteens from a small stream that fed into the River Jordan. I asked Nathan and Jacob if they also thought that the sounds of the enemy artillery had died down.

"I think so, now that you mention it," Jacob said, wiping flies off his face for the thousandth time that morning. "Maybe the Turks have finally retreated from around here."

Nathan shrugged. "Or they're waiting up in the cliffs ahead, ready to ambush us."

But Jacob was nearer the truth. Most of the enemy troops in the area had indeed pulled back to the north, a fact that was later confirmed after we had interrogated a wounded enemy soldier.

Lieutenants Jabotinsky and Barnes were marching at the head of our column, and as soon as we reached the ford at Umm Es Shert we set up our eight Lewis machine guns in positions so that we covered both sides of the River Jordan. Soon after we had taken control of the ford, some Turkish troops in the hills started firing down at us.

"Get your heads down!" a sergeant shouted at us. His order was not necessary: we had already ducked down and dived for cover. Small puffs of dirt and dust rose from where their bullets fell around us, while a few ricocheted off the surrounding rocks into the distance with a metallic pinging noise. One of our men, a new recruit who had joined us in Jerusalem, was hit in the leg by a ricocheting bullet, but no one else was hit. At first it was hard to see where the firing came from, but soon we could make out the muzzle flashes of their guns and began to return their fire. Our Lewis guns let off a few long bursts into the hills and the enemy shooting from the hilltops stopped.

"That's it?" Jacob asked after a few minutes of tense silence.

"Looks like it. But wait a bit longer."

A soldier behind me stood up but was pulled down by a friend. "Get down! *Savlanut*, hold on," he said in Hebrew. "This could be a trap."

We waited there, patient and tense. It was hard, as the flies were out now in full force, making all of us rub our faces. The buzzing pests tried to get into our eyes and noses, and even inside our collars. It was too much for one of the men. Suddenly he got up and started shouting, "To hell with you!" at the distant Turks. The man nearest to him pulled him down but it was too late. We heard the sharp crack of a single bullet and the shouting man fell on the spot and lay there without moving. A red stain immediately spread out all over his chest and the dusty ground he lay on. We did not dare move to try to help him. There was no point. We could see that he was dead. It was clear that we were still well within range of the Turkish snipers. We fired some long bursts at them again but they did not reply, so we lay still and waited. We were now so tense that we ignored the flies and just lay there alert, ready for another outburst. It never came.

Suddenly from behind us we could hear the sounds of heavy army boots crunching over the rocky ground. We turned around, rifles at the ready, and were relieved to see that they were our men. They were the scouts Barnes had sent into the hills to report on the Turks – how many there were and where they were situated. They reported that the enemy had cleared out since killing our shouting soldier and had left only their dead and wounded behind.

"It seems that Sam was shot by a wounded sniper," I said to Nathan. "What a way to go."

Before we moved off, we buried Sam Levine in a grave, piling rocks over it to make a small cairn. We wedged a small wooden board with his name, rank, army number and date of death into the rocks. We then stood around while his best friend said *Kaddish* over him.

So the ford at Umm Es Shert was ours. The Turks had fled and we had captured it with hardly any casualties. A message was sent to General Chaytor's headquarters and soon we saw a group of Australian cavalrymen crossing the River Jordan on their way to Es Salt. Wagon trains and camels followed and, we, the dusty and dirty fighters of the Jewish Legion, felt proud and happy that we had done our bit in chasing the Turks out of this important section of the Jordan Valley.

Later we learned that the Anzac cavalry had cut the enemy to shreds; those who were captured were sent back to us as prisoners of war.

"Look at them," I said to Nathan, as we were herding them into the barbed-wire compounds. "They look more like beggars and tramps than soldiers. Just look at those torn and tatty uniforms."

"Yes. And they stink."

"Well, not for long," a passing sergeant said. "They're going to be washed and disinfected soon. But just don't get too close to them or you'll get what they've got."

He was right. Soon after, the prisoners were washed and disinfected and then given some old British army uniforms that had been dyed black. However, over the next few days quite a few of them died of their wounds, disease and malnutrition. They were buried in a special area by their comrades. Of course we kept our distance from them, but I noticed that as the days passed, our prisoners began to look less like skeletons and more like ordinary people.

One day Jacob called me to come over to one of the prisoner compounds.

"David," he said, "there are some Turks in there who say they are Jewish."

"What do you mean, Jewish? What are Jews doing in the Turkish army?"

"They say they were forced to join the army back home, and there's one who even says he's a Russian Jew."

"So what's he doing in the Turkish army?" I repeated.

Jacob shrugged. "I don't know but luckily he speaks a little Yiddish. All he told me was that one day when he was in Turkey on a business trip, the Turks forced him to join their army."

"Sounds like the press-gangs they used to have in England years ago. You know, when they had to force men to join the army to fight Napoleon," I said.

"Right. Well, let's go and see what this is all about."

When we got to the compound half a dozen prisoners pushed their way forward to the barbed wire. Three of them immediately started talking in Hebrew.

"*Anachnu Yehudim*, we're Jewish. *Anachnu me'Istanbul*, we're from Istanbul."

Two others started talking in Yiddish, and Jacob, whose Yiddish was better than mine, asked them who they were and what they were doing in the Turkish army.

"And what about him?" I asked, pointing to a short soldier in a black POW uniform who was standing to the side and watching us very intently. "Is he also Jewish?"

They shrugged. They didn't know. I motioned to him to join the others.

"*Ata Yehudi?* Are you Jewish?" I asked.

He looked at me blankly.

"*Du bist a Yid?*" Jacob asked him in Yiddish. He still looked at me blankly and then looked down at the scruffy boots on his feet.

"Wait a minute, Jacob. I have an idea." I looked at him. "*Shema Yisrael*, hear O Israel," I said.

He looked up and a huge smile spread across his scrawny face. "*Hashem Elokenu, Hashem echad*, the Lord is our God, the Lord is one," he continued the ancient Jewish prayer quietly without any hesitation.

"He's Jewish, all right," I said. "But I don't know where he's from. Come on, Jacob. Let's go and report this. I don't think it's a good idea for the Jewish prisoners to be kept together with the rest of the Turks."

Our officers agreed with us and soon the Jewish prisoners were taken out of their compounds and put in separate ones.

"That's all very well," Jacob said, "but why do we have to keep them as prisoners?"

"I suppose they're still Turkish soldiers," Nathan replied, "even if they are Jewish POWs."

"But they're Jewish. And we're supposed to be saving the Holy Land for the Jews, for us," I said. "You know, *Kol Yisrael arevim zeh lazeh*, all Jews are responsible for one another."

"You're right, David. But I suppose that in the eyes of the top brass they're still enemy soldiers, even if they are prisoners. And remember, my friend, when all's said and done, we're a part of the British army, not our own Jewish army."

I had to agree even though I was not happy about this. Then suddenly an idea flashed into my head.

"What if they wanted to join us, the Legion? Wouldn't the British army then have to release them?"

"I don't know," Jacob said. "It would depend on what the top brass think. They might see them as possible Turkish spies."

But clearly I was not the only one who had had this idea. Some time later, Jacob found me in my tent writing letters home and to Yehudit. I was really missing her and hoped that there would be a letter from her when we got back to base.

"Listen, Mister Romeo Levi, the Brits have decided to accept about ninety of the Turkish Jewish prisoners we caught into the Legion. They checked them out to see if they were spies or not and now they're going to be part of the new 40th Battalion." Here they joined about a thousand Jews from Eretz Israel who had also recently joined the Legion, after having heard of our successes against the Turks.

It was also about this time that a large parade was organized, and Lieutenant Jabotinsky, as our commander, was awarded a medal in recognition of the Legion's contribution to the war effort. Major General Chaytor, in his thick Australian accent, also praised us, saying, "By forcing the Jordan fords, you helped in no small measure to win the great victory gained at Damascus."

We all felt very proud of having taken part in this but at the same time we felt very sad about our fallen comrades who were no longer with us. A few days later we heard that our rival battalion, the 39th, under the command of Colonel Margolin, had managed to capture Es Salt, an important strategic site north of the Dead Sea.

They had had a tough time getting there as they had lost their way in the desert and had accidentally headed north for the Damiah Bridge instead. Much valuable time had been wasted and after discovering their mistake, they had to make their way to the newly named Allenby Bridge to the south. This extra marching in the desert had been especially hard on some of the men who were suffering from fever.

A friend in the 39th told me that the Turks had used the same tactics on them as they had on us and had set fire to the area as they were retreating. As a result, huge clouds of black smoke rose from the burning fields of thornbush, causing the 39th to move as slowly as we had done. This, together with the intense heat of the Jordan Valley, had made it even tougher on the men, especially for those whose water bottles had run out. He said that the smoke was so thick that, at times, they thought that they had gotten lost as they climbed up the desert heights.

Colonel Margolin was ordered to take command of Es Salt and the battalion remained there for five days. They were then given the nasty job of keeping the local Bedouin tribesmen away from the area. Apparently both sides, we and the Turks, hated the Bedouin even more than each other. These desert tribesmen would descend from the hills like vultures and strip any corpses of their uniforms. They would grab rifles and any other military equipment left lying on the battlefield and even their women would join in these scavenging operations.

It was about this time that the British forces, including the Jewish Legion, faced the Turks on opposing sides of the Jordan Valley, and our battalion earned a good name for the number of prisoners we managed to take. We would set out on night patrols, and since many of us knew some German and some Turkish (especially those of us who had fought with the ZMC at Gallipoli), we would persuade the poorly fed enemy troops to surrender.

We often did this by telling them of our good food supplies and that they would be out of the fighting. You can imagine how surprised we were when we discovered that many of our prisoners were Jews who had been forced to serve in the Turkish army.

All of our prisoners, Jewish or not, were in a terrible state. They stank, their uniforms were in rags and their boots were completely worn out. No wonder they were exhausted, and sick and tired of the whole war. Many of them surrendered quite happily to us and said that they were as much afraid of their Turkish officers as they were of the Bedouin who roamed the hills and killed off any stragglers for their rifles and ammunition.

By the time we were ordered to move back to Jerusalem from the Jordan Valley at the beginning of October 1918, the British army and the Anzac forces under General Chaytor had taken about eleven thousand enemy soldiers as prisoners. Most of these were Turkish, but there were also quite a few Germans among them. They had served as instructors and now, hearing how we had treated our captured Turkish Jewish prisoners, some of the Germans tried to trick us into thinking that they too were Jewish by speaking an unconvincing sort of pidgin Yiddish.

The march back to Jerusalem was just as hard as the descent into the Jordan Valley had been a few weeks earlier. We of the 38th were responsible for one thousand POWs and the 39th were responsible for another thousand. We set out from Shunit Namrin and the 39th headed west from Es Salt. We all plodded along, the silence being broken by the sounds of our boots on the hot roads and the creaking of our ammunition belts and other military equipment we had to carry. Every so often a soldier or prisoner would fall, gasping for air or water, and lie sprawled out on the rough sand-colored rocks at the side of the road. Sometimes friends tried to help by carrying them or by giving up some of their own precious supply of water, but often this help came too late, especially for the prisoners who were in a terrible state even before we had started the steep climb up from Jericho to Jerusalem. Many of them were suffering from malaria and the fever weakened them even more.

"David," Jacob said to me panting, his face bright red from the effort he was making, "I don't think I'm going to make it. I'm feeling terrible. My legs feel all soft and rubbery."

"Take this stick. It should help you."

Fortunately it did, but not everyone was so lucky. By the time we had reached the top of the high ridge on which Jerusalem sits, most of the men of the two battalions and their prisoners were in a bad way. Many of those who had fallen by the way were later picked up by trucks dispatched for this purpose, but for some of the fallen this was too late.

We had a few days' rest in Jerusalem, but this time there was no sightseeing. The only thing that Nathan, Jacob and I wanted to do was to eat, drink and sleep. Luckily some of the Jewish women of Jerusalem looked after us. Later we heard that Colonel Patterson had been very angry with his superiors, accusing them of discriminating against his forces, simply because they were Jewish. He told them in no uncertain terms that the top brass had not provided him with enough medical aid and supplies. He felt that those above him had betrayed him, especially as he felt very proud of what we had achieved.

On October 9, Jacob walked into the tent I shared with him and Nathan and a couple of others and interrupted our card game with the latest news.

"Listen, you lot, I've just heard we're to be sent to Lod."

"That's great," I said, grinning. "We won't be far from home. We'll be able to see our families."

"You mean your Yehudit, you love-struck soldier," someone laughed at me.

But Nathan was less happy. "What?" he groaned. "Another long cross-country march?"

"Not this time. The British army is going to spoil us for once. We're going by train."

"But there are still quite a lot of men who are sick here," Jacob said. "They're in no state to travel."

"I know that. I've heard that they're going to be left behind and then will be sent on later."

But that was not to be. Colonel Margolin of the 39th refused to leave anyone behind in Jerusalem, and so it was only after a five-day delay that both battalions, we and the 39th, entrained for Lod.

We stayed at the huge base at Sarafend, near Lod, but despite our requests, we were not allowed to go home even for a few hours. While we were there, "cooling our heels," as Nathan put it, twenty of our men died of malaria. When I heard this I thought it was so unfair. Some of them, including Jake Gold and Hymie Levinson, who had served with me in the ZMC and been through so much over the past three years – Egypt, Gallipoli, Plymouth, Italy and Umm Es Shert – had died so near home, and all because of some stupid mosquito! There was just no logic to it all.

It was while we were at Sarafend that we heard that Allenby, the victorious general who had beaten the Turks at Gaza, Beersheva and Jerusalem, had now beaten them once again and was in control of most of the north. After some tough fighting in the Jordan and Jezreel Valleys, he had entered the ancient city of Damascus on the first day of October. But he did not stop there. Living up to his nickname, "The Bull" had pushed his men even further north and finished his campaign three weeks later when he captured the northern Syrian town of Aleppo. When we heard this, we knew that for us the war was over. Eretz Israel had a new master. The Turks (or to be historically correct, the Ottomans), who had occupied our homeland for the past four hundred years, were to give way to the British.

Now it was their turn to control our destiny. I wondered when it would be ours.

"When will we be independent? You know, a Jewish country with its own government and army," I asked Nathan.

"I don't know," he shrugged. "But I hope the British will be better for us than the Turks."

"And I hope that we'll see an independent Jewish country within our own lifetime," I said.

He nodded in agreement.

It was only months later that I learned what we had been a part of. When you are fighting and taking part in a battle, unless you are a general or one of the top brass, you never see the whole picture. You are too busy following orders, dodging bullets or scratching mosquito bites to see what is happening all around you.

It seems that we had played no mean part in Allenby's plan to beat the Turks in Palestine. We had been part of a huge British army trap. We had closed in on the enemy while fighting east of the Dead Sea at Es Salt and Umm Es Shert. It is true that it took us six weeks to beat the Turks but, when we did, we took over seventy thousand of them prisoner, as well as capturing several hundred pieces of artillery, rifles and machine guns. All this, of course, was in addition to knowing that we had thrown the enemy out of our ancient capital, Jerusalem, forever and that hundreds of years of Ottoman rule had finally come to an end. It certainly was a good feeling to know that I had played a part, however small, in all that!

CHAPTER TWELVE
Armistice and Demobilization

I am glad we did not have to stay at Sarafend for long. In the first week of November 1918 we were given orders to proceed to Rafa, in Egypt. This was good news because it meant that we were to be sent to a rest camp and, after all our fighting the Turks and the mosquitoes, a good long rest was what we all needed.

The other piece of good news was that I received a long letter from Yehudit. The company clerk brought it over to me and I sat down under a spreading tree and began to read it.

My dearest David,

It seems so long since I've heard from you (even though I received your last letter yesterday) and I miss you so much. Yes, the old saying "Absence makes the heart grow fonder" is true. Very true. All I can say is now that you are here in Eretz Israel I hope we will soon be together again.

Anyway I'll stop babbling on and let you know about some of the things that have been happening here while you've been away. So many things have happened since I last wrote to you in England and I'm sure you must have heard some of what I'm going to tell you before, but here goes.

Life here under the Turks was very tough and I was so proud that you and the ZMC and the Brits managed to throw them and their Austrian supporters out of the country. We really suffered from starvation even though the cruel Hassan Bey was replaced by Governor Ahmed Shukri.

In the north, some people, especially the Aaronsohn family and their friends, set up an anti-Turkish spy ring called NILI. I don't know much about it but they managed to smuggle information to the British. The

Turks found a NILI carrier pigeon with a note tied to its foot and then killed and tortured many of the NILI members, most of whom lived in or near Zichron Ya'acov. Some people here were against the NILI and said it was a dangerous and irresponsible organization because it gave the Turks an excuse to act even tougher against the rest of us.

In addition, there have been several plagues of locusts (that's what comes of living in the Land of the Bible!) and they caused great damage. Mother complained about the cost of food becoming even more expensive, but of course there was nothing we could do about it.

Just before Passover last year, the Turks expelled many people from Tel Aviv and Jaffa, including us! That is why a couple of my letters had Kfar Saba written at the top. I didn't want to tell you why as sometimes the Turks opened our mail. We spent some time in this little village, but later we managed to get back to our old house. It was in a filthy and disgusting state. Words were written all over the walls in the front room, most of the windows had been broken, and even my collection of dolls and dry flowers had been wrecked!

But, my dearest David, not all the news is bad. Your family and mine are well, and if you haven't heard, your father was allowed to come home from Egypt!!! That night, your mother and mine brought out all their secret reserves of food (trust the Jewish mothers!) and we had a noisy celebration party. Your father drank a bit too much but otherwise he looks all right even though he lost a bit of weight there and his hair has gone greyer. He has even learned how to swear in Arabic! Who would believe it? Your ever-respectable father!

Now that you are so near (and yet so far) I am looking forward like mad to seeing you again. Can't you get any leave at least for a day or so? Please please try. Tell your commander you have to go home and see your sick old grandmother, or something like that. Aren't Jewish officers supposed to be worried about their men and their families? Just try to think of a good excuse. I'm waiting for you and miss you so much.

I must finish this and rush off to the post office before it closes. Please

CHAPTER TWELVE: ARMISTICE AND DEMOBILIZATION

please look after yourself. You've been through so much and I don't want anything to happen to you now, not even a scratch!
    Best wishes to Nathan and Jacob.
    I miss you lots and lots.
    Love,
    Y.

I felt great, especially after reading that my father had returned home safe and sound, and that Yehudit had signed her letter again: "Love, Y." Unfortunately, however, all my attempts at getting leave were fruitless; we would have to wait yet a while longer before we would be able to see each other again.

    Meanwhile it was at least a relief to be out of combat. Our new "home," Rafa, did not look like much of a rest camp, especially as it had been set up in the middle of a desert-like area, but we did not care. Here we could relax, play football and cricket, take part in boxing matches, or just lie around, read and write letters home. Many of our sporting activities were against the friendly Anzac soldiers who'd also been sent there to rest.

    One day as Nathan and I were getting ready for a soccer match – he was playing center forward and I was to play goalie – Jacob ran over to tell us that that afternoon, General Chaytor of the Australian army would be inspecting the Legion. A parade would be organized and some of our officers and men were going to be presented with medals.

    That afternoon, as we stood assembled on three sides of the parade ground, General Chaytor took the salute, shook hands with Lieutenant Colonel Patterson and started to speak. I cannot remember everything he said, but I do remember him saying that he wanted us to know that he appreciated our efforts on the Mellaha front near the Dead Sea where we had defeated the Turks. He praised our success at the Umm Es Shert ford which had allowed his cavalry to push on to Es Salt and capture many of the enemy troops as well as a large quantity of their guns and ammunition. He also mentioned our help in supporting his successful attack on Rabbath Amman and his army's destruction of the Turkish Fourth Army. He finished his speech saying that we of the Jewish Legion had done very well and, in recognition of his appreciation, he wished to present several of us with medals.

We felt very proud as Major Neil was awarded the Distinguished Service Order (DSO), and watched carefully as the enameled white Maltese cross, edged in gold with a crown in the center and a red and blue ribbon, was pinned onto his chest. Five captains and lieutenants were awarded the Military Cross, and seven other soldiers received other decorations.

"What! Don't I get one?" Nathan whispered. "You know, for fighting off hordes of enemy mosquitoes in the Jordan Valley."

"No," I whispered back, "'cause if you get a medal for that, we'd all have to get one at least, if not a whole sack of them."

Other officers and men were informed that although they would not receive any medals, their heroic efforts were to be officially praised and were to be mentioned in dispatches. Their names would be forwarded to General Allenby and the War Office in London.

A few days later we were ordered to assemble on the parade ground again, and there Colonel Patterson informed us that the war was officially over. "An armistice agreement was signed with the German army, which surrendered two hours ago. This took place on the Western Front in France, at 1100 hours," he announced. "But before we break out into any form of celebration, we will observe a minute's silence to remember our fallen comrades."

CHAPTER TWELVE: ARMISTICE AND DEMOBILIZATION   125

Naturally we were pleased to hear that the war was over and I thought about Benny Goldman and Sam Levine who had died what seemed to be especially pointless deaths at Gallipoli and here in the Jordan Valley. Then I started thinking about the future. What would happen to us and how long would we have to stay in the army? Some of us, like Nathan, Jacob and myself, had been in uniform since the ZMC had been established over three years earlier. We had fought at Gallipoli, trained at Plymouth and fought again in the deserts around Amman and the Dead Sea. To be honest, we had had enough. It was time to go home. When would we be demobbed, or demobilized, to use the official phrase?

We heard later that the top brass in the British army were not happy about sending us to serve in the towns and cities in Palestine. Perhaps they were worried that we'd join up with the civilian Jewish population who were clamoring for some sort of independence. And so they separated us: the 38th were to stay in Rafah, near Gaza, the 39th were to stay in their camp at Sarafend, and the newly formed 40th were to remain in Egypt to be employed looking after the Egyptian prisoners of war. Of the three battalions, the 40th were the most disappointed. They had hoped to take part in the fighting as we had and so enjoy some of the glory in ridding the Holy Land of the hated Turks. But the armistice had overtaken them and so they had to remain in Egypt until the army decided what it was going to do with them.

At about the same time, Allenby received orders from London that he was to send over a thousand of the most recent American volunteers to join up with our other Legionnaires in Egypt. They would become our fourth battalion, the 42nd. And while this was happening, two thousand more volunteers from England and the United States, under the command of Colonel

Samuel, were waiting in Plymouth for their marching orders. But they would have to continue waiting in England.

This, then, was our situation at the end of 1918. We – the British, the Americans and the French – had won the war; the Germans had been beaten in Europe and the Turks had been thrown out of the Middle East. The Bolsheviks had gotten rid of the czar in Russia, and we were left to cool our heels in the sands and the chaos of the newly liberated Middle East.

In the meanwhile, the War Office in London was persuaded to add the name "The Judeans" to our original name, The King's Rifles. Our new badge was to be a menorah with the word *Kadima* (forward) written underneath in Hebrew.

Badge of the First "Judeans" Corps

Naturally we felt very proud about this but then Nathan asked cynically, "Yes, it looks fine, but is it going to get us home any faster?"

We were still hanging around a few months later when we were informed that we, of the Legion, were to be responsible for the security of the railroad network in Palestine. At the same time, some of our men who had come from England were demobilized, and this caused a lot of bad feeling among the Americans and Canadians. When they complained and demanded to know why they had not been demobbed as well, they were told that it was just a matter of organization and, as soon as suitable transport could be found, they too would be returning home.

CHAPTER TWELVE: ARMISTICE AND DEMOBILIZATION

It was at this point that some of the new American recruits who had arrived after the armistice were transferred from their base camp and joined us to make up our numbers. At first we were not very pleased about this, as we thought that if our numbers increased, this would give the authorities an excuse not to disband us so quickly. We also suspected that the civilian Zionist authorities in London and Jerusalem were working hand in glove with the British.

"You know what I think?" Nathan said one evening as we were sitting around one evening griping about the situation. "I think that Weizmann and those others in their nice comfy offices in London and Jerusalem are quite happy that we're still in the army. It's like we're adding strength to the Zionist movement and so we'll all have an independent Jewish country very soon."

"I wish that were the case," I added. "Then I wouldn't mind all this hanging around. But just to be kept here keeping my boots polished and my rifle clean is really getting on my nerves."

Jacob shrugged but continued polishing his boots.

In fact, the situation got so bad that, at the beginning of July, thirty-five men in the 38th declared a strike after receiving orders to send 150 men to serve as guards at two prisoner of war camps in Cairo and Alexandria. They closed themselves in their tents and refused to come out for their turn at guard duty. They were put under guard for mutiny, a crime that carries the death penalty during wartime conditions, and were then joined the next day by eighteen men of the 39th. The striking troops, led by Shmuel Yavnieli, Eliahu Golomb and Dov Hoz, declared that they had joined the Jewish Legion to rid Eretz Israel of the Turks and not to fight other battles for the British. One of our commanding officers called Scott tried to reason with the men and, after discussing the matter with General Western in Kantara, he managed to get the order sending the Legion troops to Egypt delayed.

When Jabotinsky heard about this he was very pleased. In fact he was so angry with the British army authorities, which he accused of being anti-Semitic, that he sent a letter to General Allenby himself! He said that he was the founder of the Zion Mule Corps and of the Jewish Legion and now all of his work was being smashed into smithereens because of the anti-Semitism that was now a part of the British military administration. He said the men were bitterly disappointed and desperate, as they could see how all the promises made to them were being broken.

Jabotinsky had even written to his commanding officer to say that he had heard that he, the officer, had anti-Zionism feelings; he hoped this wasn't true, and that what was happening to the Jewish troops was being done without his knowledge and support. Jabotinsky finished his letter saying that there was still an opportunity to improve this state of affairs, adding that he would be very pleased to meet with him in an effort to sort out the situation.

When we heard about Jabotinsky's letter we were very pleased, but shocked. Wow! To think that a lieutenant, and a Jewish lieutenant as well, would have the chutzpa to write a letter like that to General Allenby! We wondered what would happen. Would Jabotinsky be sent to prison for insubordination? He was not, even though Allenby had the right to punish this outspoken officer. Instead, he sent another Jewish officer to see Jabotinsky to persuade him to retract his letter. This did not work out as planned, and at the beginning of September 1919, Allenby decided to discharge Lieutenant Jabotinsky from the army.

As you can guess, the atmosphere in our camp was electric and the only thing we could talk about was the strike, or the *mered*, as we called it in Hebrew, and what the outcome might be. The tension increased day by day, and then after two weeks Lieutenant Colonel Scott received orders that we were to be sent on our original mission to Egypt, immediately! We were told that we were part of the British army and that orders had to be carried out whether we liked them or not! There was to be no discussion about the matter.

Scott even tried to ease the tension by sending the men who did not really object to carrying out this order, but Golomb, Hoz and some others would not accept this and threatened the strikebreakers. Then there were more angry arguments between the hot-headed Golomb, Hoz and their supporters, on one side, and Yitzhak Ben-Zvi, who was more moderate, on the other. He said that there was a big difference between personal objections to carrying out orders and organizing a rebellion against the authorities. Perhaps it was due to his moderate, compromising nature that Yitzhak Ben-Zvi was later to become the second president of the State of Israel. But I'm getting ahead of myself.

After many arguments, in the end Golomb and his men won. Most of us voted against being sent to Egypt. Scott was flabbergasted by this and ordered Hoz, who was a sergeant major, to read out the British army's standing orders concerning the refusal to carry out orders. Hoz read them out to us on the dusty parade ground in a sing-song mocking tone, explaining that our behavior could be punished with a life sentence and hard labor.

When he finished reading he called out, "All of you who still wish to refuse to carry out the order about going to Egypt, take one step forward." A hundred of us did so. The remaining thirty remained where they were, and after some confusion and noisy arguments, they were sent to their tents. Golomb then tried to persuade them to join the others, while Lieutenant Colonel Scott sent an urgent message to his headquarters in Kantara. His superior officers decided to be very cautious especially when they learned that we were acting in a quiet and disciplined manner. In the end, headquarters informed the unfortunate Scott that he should deal with us as he saw fit. As a result he tried to court-martial some of us, but this failed when we blocked the door and wouldn't allow the "guilty" soldiers into the courtroom.

Things were going from bad to worse and at this point the Zionist civilian authorities intervened. They sent David Eder (who later had a training farm named after him in the south of England), who arrived with the aim of bringing this impossible situation to an end as quickly and as quietly as possible. His task was made easier as Golomb and Yavnieli, the chief "troublemakers," had been sent out on an escort mission to Kantara the day before. Eder managed to restore peace and quiet, even though Golomb claimed that we had surrendered to the authorities. However, by now, it was obvious that the British had had enough of us, their Jewish soldiers, and on December 9, 1919, thirteen months after the armistice, the 39th and the 40th Battalions were disbanded and only the 38th remained.

Two months later, in February 1920, four hundred Jewish soldiers in the 38th Battalion volunteered to serve for a further three months while Jabotinsky, now independent of the British army's restrictions, took on the responsibility of setting up the Haganah, a Jewish self-defense organization in Jerusalem. He worked hard to have his organization officially recognized by the British and contacted the most important British authorities in Palestine: Major General Louis Bols and

Colonel Ronald Storrs, the military governor of Jerusalem. He even embarrassed them by asking them to supply him with arms and ammunition.

It was about this time that we received some bad news. I was sitting in an army canteen with Jacob and a few other "old-timers" like myself, talking, as old soldiers do, about past exploits and the men who had fought with us at Gallipoli and Eretz Israel, when Nathan came in with a very long face.

"Trumpeldor's dead," he said before we could ask him anything.

"What happened?"

"In Palestine. Far up in the extreme north, in the Upper Galilee."

"How?"

"It seemed that he was at this settlement up there, called Tel Hai, and some Arabs came in."

"What do you mean, they came in? Did Trumpeldor let them in?"

"I think so. It looks as though there had been some sort of fighting, you know, cowboys and Indians stuff, in the area between the Arabs and the Jewish settlers at Metulla, Kfar Giladi and Tel Hai. And then on top of this there were problems between the British and the French as to who should be in charge up there."

"So what did that have to do with Trumpeldor?" I asked.

"Well, a few days later a whole lot of armed Arabs surrounded the main building at Tel Hai. I heard that their chief tricked the Jews at Tel Hai into letting them in. They wanted to see if there were any French soldiers hiding out there."

"Why French soldiers?"

"I don't know. I just know that the Arabs up there really hated the French and wanted to kill them."

"And were there any French soldiers there?"

"I don't know. All I know is that Trumpeldor agreed to let a few of the Arabs into the courtyard. And once they were inside, they tried to take the place over. When Trumpeldor saw what was going on, he told his men to shoot the Arabs and then everyone started firing their guns."

"And was that when Trumpeldor was killed?"

"Yes, I suppose so," Nathan said, looking down. "He was shot in the stomach. I heard he died from his wounds on the way to Kfar Giladi where they were taking him for medical treatment."

"Was he the only one killed?" Jacob asked.

"No. About half a dozen others were killed with him."

We all looked down. No one had anything to say. We remembered him and how he had been our commander at Gallipoli. Nothing had been too hard for him. The fact that he had only one arm had not prevented him from doing anything and he had survived on the rocky mountainsides there as well as any of us.

"I bet he swore at the Arabs in that good ol' Russian of his," I said, half smiling, thinking about our eight months of service on the Gallipoli peninsula under his command.

"I'm sure he did," Nathan agreed. "But they said his last words were, 'No matter, it is good to die for our country.'"

"Maybe..." I said. "But do you really think he... I just...I'm not completely convinced about that one."

Jacob nodded. "Me neither. But at least it will look good if they ever write about him in the history books."

A month later we were still hanging around wondering what the future held in store when, at the beginning of April, anti-Jewish rioting broke out in Jerusalem. The British were not prepared to use us, their Jewish troops, to put down the rioters.

Later we heard that once the dust had settled, the Old City of Jerusalem looked as though a Russian-style pogrom had hit it. We were forbidden to go anywhere near the city, but a few of us did manage to sneak out and get to Jerusalem in time to help Jabotinsky and our fellow Jews there.

When the British discovered this they were furious and arrested Jabotinsky. They put him and nineteen others on trial two weeks later and our former commanding officer received a fifteen-year sentence with hard labor! The court also declared that when he had served his time in prison, he was to be removed from Palestine. The Haganah men arrested with him each received a much lighter sentence of only three years.

"It looks as though the British haven't forgiven him for what happened during our *mered*," I said.

"That's true enough," Jacob added. "And for that letter he sent to General Allenby."

Then, at the end of April 1920, it was the Galilee's turn to experience more anti-Jewish rioting. The Jewish soldiers in Eretz Israel demanded that Colonel Margolin, one of the leading commanding officers of the Jewish Legion during the First World War, send them north to help defend their fellow Jews. The colonel promised to help and, while he was trying to organize this, about half the Jewish soldiers stationed at Sarafend sneaked out of the base and made their way north. Their Jewish officers turned a blind eye to this unofficial act.

However, despite the sad state of affairs in Palestine, there was a bright light shining through this gloomy picture. Less than three months after he had been sentenced to serve fifteen years in prison, Jabotinsky was released in July 1920 on the orders of the new high commissioner for Palestine, Herbert Samuel. At about the same time most of the remaining soldiers of the Jewish Legion were demobilized and only thirty-nine

NCOs and men remained in uniform to act as the core for a new unit to be commanded by Colonel Margolin. As luck would have it, Nathan, Jacob and I were among the thirty-nine "very old timers," as we called ourselves.

"Do you remember the words of that old army song, David?" Jacob asked me when we heard the news. "Old soldiers never die. They just fade away."

And that's what we nearly did. Fade away. Nothing much happened to us for a few months. We did hear that in December 1920, Jabotinsky was working on a plan to establish a Jewish regiment in Eretz Israel, a unit to be supported by the Jewish Labor Federation; but, as far as I know, nothing came of this. Then a few months later the British government decided to adopt a plan that High Commissioner Samuel had worked out, to form a unit consisting of both Arab and Jewish troops. I thought that this was a good idea. It was intended to relieve the tension in the Holy Land but, like Jabotinsky's plan, nothing came of it.

However, despite all this, the situation remained fairly calm for a few months and then in May 1921, anti-Jewish rioting broke out in Tel Aviv-Jaffa. We were back again at the big base at Sarafend at the time and we, together with some men of the Northern Palestinian defense unit, were sent to deal with the rioters. For us, this really meant helping to defend our fellow Jews. When the British military authorities refused to give arms and support to fifty ex-Jewish Legionnaires who came forward to help us, Colonel Margolin was furious, especially when after a lot of arguing and thumping fists on tables, he was eventually issued eighteen old Turkish rifles and two hundred bullets!

Then, to make matters worse, a British colonel arrived and asked Colonel Margolin if it was true that he was in command of an unofficial unit. He then issued an order that Margolin must remain in Tel Aviv and not enter the Arab areas of Jaffa, even to rescue some of the Jews who were trapped in the southern part of the city. The colonel then confiscated some of Margolin's men's rifles. The bad situation was complicated even more when General Costello ordered Margolin to disarm the volunteer soldiers who had joined him. He also ordered our commanding officer to take us back to our base at Sarafend. And all this was happening while anti-Jewish rioting was taking place in Tel Aviv!

This was the last straw for Colonel Margolin, who resigned his commission from the British army there and then on the spot. I think the British were quite relieved about this: it saved them the embarrassment of putting a colonel and his unit on trial for insubordination.

That night as we were sitting in our tents at Sarafend regretting that we could do nothing for our fellow Jews in Tel Aviv, we talked about what would happen to us.

Jacob thought that since Margolin had resigned his commission, we old-timers would be demobilized as a way of ridding the army of this troublesome Jewish unit. I disagreed.

"Don't you see?" I said. "The British army needs us. They need soldiers who can speak English and Hebrew. And some of us can speak Arabic as well. You'll see. When the rioting is over, they'll call Margolin back and they'll take us seriously again."

But Jacob was right and I was wrong. In May 1921, the Jewish Legion was finally disbanded and we were all demobilized. The British army and the Mandatory authorities decided to run the Holy Land without our help. The Zion Mule Corps, the Jewish Legion and the Judeans were now history. After six years of "serving with the colors," Nathan, Jacob and I were civilians once again! It was a strange feeling. We had been through everything together and come through it all without being seriously wounded. We had trained at Gabbari in Egypt, fought at Gallipoli, undergone more training at Crown Hill, Plymouth, England, and taken part in the fighting at Es Salt and Umm Es Shert. On top of this we had spent two and a half years guarding the railroad network in Eretz Israel as well as getting involved in various mutinous activities.

Three months later, at the end of August 1921, Yehudit and I were married in Tel Aviv. It wasn't a very big wedding; about seventy people attended. Of course the two families came, as well as half a dozen past ZMC friends including Nathan and Jacob. After I had smashed the glass and the *sheva brachot* (seven wedding blessings) had been recited, we sat down to eat.

"Now, David," Yehudit warned, pulling me away from Nathan and Jacob. "Don't you start talking about your old ZMC days all the time with these two. You've got to meet my Uncle Solly and Aunt Sarah who have come all the way from Haifa to be here today."

Nathan slapped me on the back. "Oh, ho, David, my friend. Now you are truly married, except that from now on you'll be taking orders from Sergeant Yehudit and not from Colonel Patterson!"

My reply was to give Yehudit a big kiss and tell my two friends to go find something to eat before it was all gone. They didn't need to be told twice.

Despite my being married, I remained very friendly with my past ZMC buddies and over the next six months Yehudit and I were very happy to be able to attend their own weddings. After that we would visit each other's houses on Friday nights or on Shabbat in the afternoons and spend the time sitting in the garden or strolling along the beach talking about our work, sport and our families. However, whatever subjects we started to talk about, we invariably ended up discussing the current political and social situation in Mandatory Palestine. Whatever we disagreed on, one point united us: we were all concerned about the worsening situation that was developing in our own Tel Aviv-Jaffa area.

Perhaps in order to give us more of a sense of involvement, we volunteered to help out with the newly formed Haganah military defense organization. Originally it had been established to protect kibbutzim and other settlements from Arab attacks. But as the time passed and the attacks became more local and violent, we found ourselves spending more and more time doing guard duty and patrolling around in our own city. This we did in addition to using our past military experiences to help and train other volunteers. Although our wives were not very pleased we were spending so much of our time with the Haganah, they understood why and what we were doing and complained only when these activities interfered with family gatherings such as weddings.

The brightest spot during this difficult period was in spring 1924 when our first son was born. This chubby little bright-eyed baby was named Benny, after Benny Goldman, the first ZMC soldier who had been killed in action on board the *Hymettus*, the warship that had taken us from Egypt to Gallipoli many years before.

By the time more serious Arab rioting had broken out five years later, Benny had Daniel and Sharon, his twin brother and sister, for company and I was an officer in the Haganah.

And what did I do as an officer in the Haganah? That story, I promise, I will tell you some other day.

Afterword

Although the Zion Mule Corps, and its successor, the Jewish Legion, later known as the Judeans, lasted for only six years, it was to become the forerunner of the modern Israeli army. Even before the Jewish Legion was finally disbanded in 1921, a new Jewish self-defense organization, the Haganah, was founded in June 1920. Some ten years later, for political and ideological reasons, the Haganah split up into three smaller groups: the Haganah, the Etzel or IZL *(Irgun Zva'i Leumi)* and the Lehi *(Lohamei Herut Yisrael)*. However the original Haganah remained the largest unit of these three military forces.

As in the First World War, after much pressure from the Jewish authorities, a unit called the Jewish Brigade was set up in 1944, toward the end of the Second World War, to serve within the framework of the British army. Most of its men came from British Mandatory Palestine, and they fought against the Nazis, mainly in North Africa and northeast Italy. It was commanded by the Toronto-born Brigadier E.F. Benjamin.

After the Allied victory over the Nazis in May 1945, cooperation between the British army and its Jewish troops came to an end. The main problem was that Britain did not want to allow an independent Jewish state to come into existence. This resulted in a great deal of bad feeling and bloodshed between the two former allies as the British Mandate was eventually forced to come to an end in May 1948. All three of the above-named Jewish military groups played their part in fighting for the new country.

However, once the State of Israel had been established in 1948, and following the orders of Prime Minister Ben-Gurion, all the three splinter groups were unified again to form the present-day Israeli army, the Israel Defense Forces (IDF).

Many of the leading fighters, commanders and organizers of the country's new army as well as many of the leading Israeli politicians and administrators first gained their military and organizational experience on the battlefields of Gallipoli and Palestine some thirty years earlier with the ZMC and the Jewish Legion.

Below is a list of some of the best-known early Israeli military and civilian leaders and personalities:

Ze'ev Jabotinsky (1881–1940). After serving as one of the first organizers of the Haganah self-defense organization in 1920, Jabotinsky was sentenced to fifteen years in prison by the British, but was released soon after. He joined the Zionist Executive in 1921 but resigned two years later when he disagreed with its politics. In 1925 he formed and led the breakaway group the Union of Zionist Revisionists. When the Nazi threat in Europe became obvious, Jabotinsky called for the immediate evacuation of Jews from Eastern Europe. He became the commander of the Etzel self-defense organization in 1937. He suddenly died three years later at the age of fifty-nine, while trying to drum up support in the USA for Jews to actively take part in the fighting against the Nazis. In addition to his military and political talents, Jabotinsky was a gifted writer and translator. He wrote and spoke several languages and even translated *The Raven*, by the American writer Edgar Allan Poe, into Hebrew. Today, many important streets and buildings in Israel are named in his honor.

Joseph Trumpeldor (1880–1920). After leading the ZMC at Gallipoli and helping Jabotinsky set up the Jewish Legion, Trumpeldor returned to Russia in 1917 to establish the Zionist

Hehalutz (Pioneers) movement. Two years later he returned to Palestine and was responsible for much of the self-defense organization of the isolated settlements in the Galilee. He was killed in action, along with seven others, while defending Tel Hai from Arab marauders. His famous last words are said to have been, "It is good to die for our country." After his death Trumpeldor became recognized as a major figure of pioneering and self-defense. As a result, it has been suggested recently that the one-armed fighter (he lost his left arm fighting in the Russo-Japanese War in 1904) be honored by establishing a Trumpeldor Day in memory of this brave man and all the other Israeli soldiers who have lost limbs while fighting in the army.

Gershon Agron (1894–1959). After serving in the Jewish Legion, Gershon Agron worked in the press bureau of the Zionist Commission. He became a member of the Jewish Agency and was a delegate to the UN Conference at San Francisco in 1949. In 1932 he became the founder-editor of the *Palestine Post*, the English-language daily newspaper (which changed its name to the *Jerusalem Post* in April 1950). From 1955 until his death four years later, Agron was the mayor of Jerusalem.

David Ben-Gurion (1886–1973). After being exiled from Palestine by the Turks in 1915, David Ben-Gurion went to the USA where, together with Yitzhak Ben-Zvi, he helped to establish the Jewish Legion. He returned to Palestine in 1918 after the First World War and became deeply involved in socialist and Zionist politics, later becoming the chairman of the Jewish Agency from 1935 to 1948. With the establishment of the State of Israel, he became the first prime minister and minister of defense. Ben-Gurion remained in politics until 1970, even after he had resigned public office in 1963. He wrote many books on Zionism and history, and died at Kibbutz Sde Boker in the

Negev (Israel's southern desert). He had chosen to make his home there as a living example to the youth of Israel to settle the isolated parts of the country.

Yitzhak Ben-Zvi (1884–1963). One of the founders of the early Jewish self-defense organization *Hashomer* (1909). Like Ben-Gurion, Yitzhak Ben-Zvi was exiled from Palestine to the USA but returned in 1918 as a soldier in the Jewish Legion, an organization he had helped to establish. After the war, he became involved in socialist and Zionist politics and became chairman of the *Va'ad Le'umi* (National Council) in 1931, serving as its president from 1945 to 1948. Four years later he was elected the second president of the State of Israel. He wrote many books and articles in Russian, Yiddish and Hebrew, and today his name lives on in the Yad Ben-Zvi institute for education and historical research in Jerusalem. There are also many streets in Israel today named in his honor.

Ya'acov Dori (1899–1973). Arriving in Palestine from Russia in 1905, Dori joined the Jewish Legion after completing his studies in 1917, and became a commander in the 40th Battalion of the Jewish Legion. After the war he remained involved in military affairs, later becoming the Haganah's northern area commander in 1929. He later helped Orde Wingate train the Special Night Squads of the Haganah and during Israel's War of Independence (1948–1949) became the first chief of staff of the Israeli army. On his retirement from army life, Ya'acov Dori became the president of the Technion – Israel Institute of Technology, in Haifa.

Levi Eshkol (1895–1969). Three years after settling in Palestine in 1914, Levi Eshkol joined the Jewish Legion and after the war was a founder of Degania Bet, one of the first kibbutzim. He then became responsible for *Mekorot* – Israel National Water Company, while serving as financial advisor for the Haganah. He then rose to importance in the Labor Party and the Jewish Agency; later he became minister of finance and then prime minister and minister of defense when Ben-Gurion resigned in 1963. He was prime minister when Israel won the Six-Day War in June 1967.

Eliyahu Golomb (1893–1945). Like Yitzhak Ben-Zvi, Elihayu Golomb fought in the pre–First World War *Hashomer* defense unit. After the war he was one of the founders of the Haganah and was also involved in the efforts to defend the outpost at Tel Hai in the Upper Galilee, the site where Trumpeldor and several others were killed in 1920. In the following year, Golomb helped in the defense of Jaffa (near Tel Aviv) during the Arab riots that broke out there. After his death, his house became a military museum, while the Yad Eliyahu sports stadium was named in his honor.

Dov Hoz (1894–1941). Born in Russia, Hoz became involved with the *Hashomer* defense unit and also worked at Degania, one of the first kibbutzim. At the beginning of the first part of the First World War, Hoz, like many Palestinian and Turkish Jews, served in the Turkish army, but then deserted and was sentenced to death in absentia. He escaped back to Palestine where he joined the Jewish Legion. After the war he became involved in socialist politics and the Haganah. In 1941 he was killed in a car crash together with some members of his family. Today, Sde Dov (Tel Aviv's local airport) and Kibbutz Dorot are named in his honor.

Dov Joseph (1899–1980). Born in Montreal, Canada, Dov Joseph arrived in Palestine in 1918 as a volunteer with the

Jewish Legion. After the war he acted as a legal advisor to the Jewish Agency and also defended members of the Haganah in British Mandatory courts. During the War of Independence (1948–1949), he became the military governor of Jerusalem when the Arabs laid siege to the capital city. Later he held several ministerial posts including the minister for trade and industry and the minister of justice.

Berl Katznelson (1887–1944). After serving in the Jewish Legion from 1918 to 1920, Berl Katznelson was one of the founders of the *Histadrut*, the Israeli trade union organization. He then acted as the chief editor of *Davar*, the trade unions' daily newspaper, until his death in 1944.

Eliezer Margolin (1895–1944). After the Jewish Legion was disbanded, Eliezer Margolin, the commander of the 39th Royal Fusiliers, managed, against the wishes of his superiors, to obtain British arms and supplies for the Jewish self-defense organization. As a result, he was forced to resign from the British army and returned to his native Australia. After his death his body was brought back and reburied in a military funeral in Israel.

Nehemiah Rabin (1886–1971). Born in the Ukraine as Nehemiah Rubitzov, he moved to the USA where he joined the Jewish Legion in 1917, arriving in Palestine toward the end of the First World War. After the war he worked in the electric company and was active in the Metal Workers' Union. He married Rosa Cohen, one of the first Haganah volunteers, in 1921 and their son Yitzhak was born the following year. Yitzhak was destined to become the chief of staff of the Israeli army during the Six-Day War, (1967). Later he entered politics, twice becoming the prime minister. He was assassinated by a right-wing fanatic at a peace rally in Tel Aviv on November 4, 1995.

Other Jewish Legionnaires who contributed to the new State of Israel included **Thomas Cousins,** who became a paymaster in the Israeli Police. *Julius Jacobs* became a secretary of the Zionist Executive and also the secretary of the Jewish Music Society. Unfortunately, he was killed when the King David Hotel in Jerusalem was bombed in July 1946 in an attack on the British Mandatory offices there by members of the Etzel. **Leon Roth,** a librarian in the Legion, became a professor of philosophy at the Hebrew University in Jerusalem, while **Horace Samuel** later became an Israeli writer and an important attorney. *Isaac Olshan* became one of the first justices in the Supreme Court of Israel and then served as its president from 1953 to 1965. He also played an active role in the trial in 1961 of the Nazi leader Adolf Eichmann.

The following are two of the most important non-Jews who were involved with the ZMC and the Jewish Legion.

Edmund H.H. Allenby (1861–1936). After failing to follow up a successful attack on the Western Front at Arras in France in 1917, General Allenby was sent to command the British forces in Egypt. He beat the Turks at Gaza, Beersheva and Jerusalem, and then routed them at Damascus and Aleppo. In 1919 he was promoted to field marshal and became the high commissioner of Egypt and the Sudan. Allenby was present at the opening ceremony of the Hebrew University campus on Mount Scopus, Jerusalem, in 1925. He died in May 1936 and many streets in Jerusalem and other cities in Israel today are named in honor of the general who defeated the Turks in Jerusalem and Palestine during the First World War.

John Henry Patterson (1867–1947). Four years after returning to England following the First World War, Colonel John

H. Patterson published his memoirs, *With the Judeans in the Palestine Campaign*, in 1922. This was the companion volume to his book *With the Zionists in Gallipoli*, published in 1916. Patterson remained in contact with the Zionist movement and even encouraged his fellow First World War officer and commander Ze'ev Jabotinsky to establish a Jewish army to fight the Nazis during the Second World War. Today, several roads in Israel are named after this British commander of the Zion Mule Corps and the Jewish Legion who identified himself so passionately with the Zionist cause and his international battalions of Jewish soldiers.

About the Author

Born and educated in England, D. Lawrence-Young arrived in Israel in 1968. Since then he has spent most of his time lecturing and teaching English and history in high schools and universities. He loves researching and writing about military history and Shakespeare. He served eighteen years in the armored infantry reserves in the Israeli army. A published (USA) and exhibited (UK & Jerusalem) photographer, he also plays the clarinet (badly), and lives in Jerusalem. He is married with three children.